"Jeremy Treat wants us to reflect deeply on the beauty of the cross. He wants us to see that the good news is much bigger than we thought, that reconciliation is further flung than we dared imagine, that the Savior to whom we are united is no less than the victorious King of all things. I can't imagine a more trustworthy guide to show us this view. With the skill of a scholar and the prose of a pastor, he takes us to the mountaintop and invites us to gaze on our great assurance."

Jen Wilkin, author; Bible teacher

"Jeremy Treat has written a brilliant yet accessible introduction to the doctrine of the atonement. He shows what Jesus's cross is about, how the cross saves, why it matters, and how it relates to the Christian life. This is a learned yet eminently readable book on a complex topic. A great starting place for anyone who wants to wrestle with the meaning of the cross and how it relates to theology as a whole."

Michael F. Bird, Academic Dean and Lecturer in New Testament, Ridley College, Melbourne

"Jeremy Treat reminds us of what every thoughtful Christian should know about the atonement while calling us to understand the cross, to worship, and to pick up our cross and follow the Master."

D. A. Carson, Cofounder and Theologian-at-Large, The Gospel Coalition

"Jeremy Treat is a model pastor-theologian. He lives and ministers in the heart of Los Angeles, one of the most dynamic, complex, and influential cities in the world. But his context hasn't tempted him to shrink away from offering the church robust teaching and theological substance. In *The Atonement*, we see Treat's pastoral heart and scholarly mind on full display. He invites us to revel in the glory of Christ crucified, explore the cross in all its profundity and life-changing potency, and return to it again and again as fuel for worship and whole-life discipleship. This is a thoughtful and accessible reflection on the heart of the gospel, indeed the heart of God. Highly recommended!"

Todd Wilson, Cofounder and President, The Center for Pastor Theologians

T0028409

"This is a master class in short, clear, and accessible systematic theology. Jeremy Treat shows us why we need to see the atonement from numerous angles to fully grasp its beauty—and then he shows us how, with a clear exposition that maintains both coherence and practical application. A superb introduction."

Andrew Wilson, Teaching Pastor, King's Church London

"Jeremy Treat represents the best of a new generation of pastor-theologians: deep but easily accessible, faithful but not shrill, cross-centered but not neglectful of the kingdom. Here is an atonement doctrine for the church—and for the world."

Joshua M. McNall, Associate Professor of Pastoral Theology, Oklahoma Wesleyan University; author, *The Mosaic of Atonement* and *How Jesus Saves*

"Evangelicals are a people of the cross—but do we understand the fullness of what this means? Jeremy Treat invites us into a rich, complex, and unified account of Jesus's atoning work—one that we can spend a lifetime meditating on and that can guide not only our study of Scripture and theology but also of the life of the church."

Adam J. Johnson, Associate Professor of Theology, Torrey Honors College, Biola University

The Atonement

SHORT STUDIES IN SYSTEMATIC THEOLOGY

Edited by Graham A. Cole and Oren R. Martin

The Atonement

An Introduction

Jeremy Treat

WHEATON, ILLINOIS

Trade paperback ISBN: 978-1-4335-7569-3
ePub ISBN: 978-1-4335-7572-3
PDF ISBN: 978-1-4335-7569-3

Library of Congress Cataloging-in-Publication Data

Names: Treat, Jeremy R., 1980- author.
Title: The Atonement : an introduction / Jeremy Treat.
Description: Wheaton, Illinois : Crossway, [2023] | Series: Short studies in systematic theology | Includes bibliographical references and index.
Identifiers: LCCN 2022044542 (print) | LCCN 2022044543 (ebook) | ISBN 9781433575693 (trade paperback) | ISBN 9781433575693 (pdf) | ISBN 9781433575723 (epub)
Subjects: LCSH: Atonement.
Classification: LCC BT265.3 .T74 2023 (print) | LCC BT265.3 (ebook) | DDC 232/.3—dc23/eng/20230412
LC record available at https://lccn.loc.gov/2022044542
LC ebook record available at https://lccn.loc.gov/2022044543

To my mother, Joyce Treat

Contents

Series Preface

The ancient Greek thinker Heraclitus reputedly said that the thinker has to listen to the essence of things. A series of theological studies dealing with the traditional topics that make up systematic theology needs to do just that. Accordingly, in each of these studies, a theologian addresses the essence of a doctrine. This series thus aims to present short studies in theology that are attuned to both the Christian tradition and contemporary theology in order to equip the church to faithfully understand, love, teach, and apply what God has revealed in Scripture about a variety of topics. What may be lost in comprehensiveness can be gained through what John Calvin, in the dedicatory epistle of his commentary on Romans, called "lucid brevity."

Of course, a thorough study of any doctrine will be longer rather than shorter, as there are two millennia of confession, discussion, and debate with which to interact. As a result, a short study needs to be more selective but deftly so. Thankfully, the contributors to this series have the ability to be brief yet accurate. The key aim is that the simpler is not to morph into the simplistic. The test is whether the topic of a short study, when further studied in depth, requires some unlearning to take place. The simple can be amplified. The simplistic needs to be corrected. As editors, we believe that the volumes in this series pass that test.

While the specific focus varies, each volume (1) introduces the doctrine, (2) sets it in context, (3) develops it from Scripture, (4) draws the various threads together, and (5) brings it to bear on the Christian life. It is our prayer, then, that this series will assist the church to delight in her triune God by thinking his thoughts—which he has graciously revealed in his written word, which testifies to his living Word, Jesus Christ—after him in the powerful working of his Spirit.

Graham A. Cole and Oren R. Martin

Acknowledgments

My life has been deeply impacted by the people who have taught me about the cross and even more by those who have lived the way of the cross. I am especially grateful for my family. My wife Tiffany is my best friend and my greatest support. Nothing I do in ministry lacks her influence. My daughters—Ashlyn, Lauryn, Evelyn, and Katelyn—are the greatest joy in my life. I hope they read this book someday. But even more, I hope they think I am a better dad than author.

I'm also filled with gratitude for my church family, Reality LA. This book has been shaped not only by study and research but also by preaching the cross and shepherding people at the foot of the cross. I'm honored to be a part of such a faithful church, let alone to be one of its pastors.

Several people contributed directly to this book. Many thanks to Uche Anizor, Hank Voss, Fred Sanders, Matt Jensen, Adam Johnson, Derek Rishmawy, and Bijan Mirtolooi, who read early drafts and gave helpful feedback. Graham Cole and Oren Martin have been wonderful general editors, and Chris Cowan's editorial insight enhanced the manuscript significantly.

I dedicate this book to my mother, Joyce Treat. My mom is the embodiment of grace and grit. Not only has she taught me about the love of God, but she has also modeled a cross-shaped life of humility, sacrifice, and love. I would not be who I am apart from God's cruciform grace at work in and through my mother.

Ultimately, I give all glory to God. For me, the cross is not merely a topic to be studied; it is good news that has renewed my life. My prayer is that this book helps the church understand the depths of the gospel so that we might truly live for the glory of God.

Introduction

The Foolishness of the Gospel

For the word of the cross is folly to those who are perishing,
but to us who are being saved it is the power of God.
1 CORINTHIANS 1:18

The Lord's plan for dealing with sin is shocking in
its unexpectedness. It will not involve force or some
military champion imposing righteousness on the people.
Rather, the Lord's solution to sin is for his servant
to take human sin on himself and to offer himself
as a sacrifice of atonement for the sins of others.[1]
PAULSON PULIKOTTIL

The good news of Christ crucified was being proclaimed in the heart of Los Angeles, but I was hearing it from a different perspective than ever before. I had the week off from preaching, so I sat with our congregation, listening to one of my fellow pastors preach 1 Corinthians 2 on the cross of Christ:

---

1. Paulson Pulikottil, "Isaiah," in *South Asia Bible Commentary*, ed. Brian Wintle (Grand Rapids, MI: Zondervan, 2015), 906.

"I decided to know nothing among you except Jesus Christ and him crucified" (1 Cor. 2:2). I had heard the words before, but as I listened on this day my eyes were fixed not on the preacher, nor on the young creatives surrounding me, but on the scar-laden head of the man sitting directly in front of me.

Like railroad tracks traversing the desolate land of his scalp, each scar told a story of pain and loss. And since this man was a part of our church, I knew the stories all too well. The first scar was from surgery at age six shortly after his childhood innocence was shattered by the words "brain cancer." The next scar came at age thirty-four when the cancer returned, and another scar was added just a few months later when an additional surgery was necessary. The most recent scar came from removing two glioblastoma tumors from the brain. After a week of chemotherapy, he had saved up all his energy to come to church. And while I trust that he was comforted by the sermon on the cross, he himself was a living illustration to our church of its meaning: God's "power is made perfect in weakness" (2 Cor. 12:9). From one perspective, people merely saw the scars, the frailty, the weakness. But from another perspective, this man's greatest problem in life had already been solved, his future hope was completely secure, and he was presently being transformed from one degree of glory to the next in a way that would make the angels blush. "The word of the cross is folly to those who are perishing, but to us who are being saved it is the power of God" (1 Cor. 1:18).

As I looked around the congregation, I realized that we are not all that different from our friend with cancer. We are all wounded; our scars are just not as visible. We are all dying; we simply have not been told how much time we have. We have all fallen short of the glory of God and experienced the pain from our own sin and the sins of others. Yet, in Christ crucified, there is the hope of complete and utter renewal. In the crucified

Nazarene is the power for healing, forgiveness, and reconciliation—not only for one man, and not only for our church in Los Angeles, but also for the whole world.

As followers of Jesus, we cling to the truth that God is making all things new by grace. But he is not doing it from afar. The Father has sent the Son in the power of the Spirit with a mission to ransom sinners and renew creation. Yet he is doing so in the most breathtaking way.

The Folly of the Cross

The crucifixion of Jesus Christ is the most significant event in the history of the world. By dying in our place, the Son of God accomplished all that is necessary for the reconciliation of sinners and the renewal of creation. But how could the death of a fairly unknown Jewish carpenter alter the course of history? Why would the crucifixion of this man—when Rome crucified tens of thousands—bring healing and hope to the lives of others? How could a gruesome execution by the state be considered *good* news? To ponder these questions is to stumble into the doctrine of atonement.

People today do not gasp at the idea of a crucifixion. We should. Crucifixion was a form of capital punishment invented to slowly torture and publicly shame criminals. As opposed to beheading, which was a quick death, crucifixion intentionally kept the victims alive long enough to plunge them into the depths of human suffering. Beyond the pain of the nails through the main arteries near the hands and feet, those hanging on the cross would spend hours or even days pulling themselves up in order to breathe, scraping their already-scourged skin on the wood of a rugged cross. So agonizing was this form of punishment that a word was later invented based on its severity: *excruciating*, which literally means "from the cross."[2]

---

2. Cicero claimed that crucifixion was the "most cruel and disgusting penalty." M. Tullius Cicero, *The Orations of Marcus Tullius Cicero*, trans. C. D. Yonge (London: George

When the Bible talks about crucifixion, however, it emphasizes not physical pain but rather social shame. Reserved for the scum of society (rebels, slaves, and outcasts), crucifixion was a public spectacle meant to humiliate and dehumanize the victim. Crucifixion usually happened along busy Roman roads, with those crucified placed in the most vulnerable position—naked, arms stretched out, and alone—in order to be taunted and mocked as they struggled for breath. Those being crucified were stripped not only of their clothes but also of their dignity. A century before Jesus, for example, a slave revolt in Rome led to six thousand people being crucified along a 130-mile stretch of a road leaving Rome.[3] The near-lifeless bodies, along with those already being eaten by vultures and vermin, served as a billboard to the world declaring the power of Rome.[4]

Since the cross was a monstrous symbol of death and defeat in the first century, it is no wonder that early Christians were mocked for worshiping a crucified Savior. The cross of Christ was "a stumbling block to Jews and folly to Gentiles" (1 Cor. 1:23). The Jews were looking for a conquering Messiah who would overthrow Rome and establish a political rule. The notion of a suffering Messiah would have been scandalous to their ears. They wanted someone who would triumph over their enemies, not be executed by them. The Gentiles (particularly

Bell and Sons, 1903), 2.5.165. Josephus referred to it as "a most miserable death." Flavius Josephus, *The Jewish War*, in *The Genuine Works of Flavius Josephus, the Jewish Historian*, trans. William Whiston (London: W. Boyer, 1737), 7.6.4. For the Jewish people, crucifixion represented the curse of God: "A hanged man is cursed by God" (Deut. 21:23). For background on crucifixion, see Martin Hengel, *Crucifixion in the Ancient World and the Folly of the Message of the Cross* (Philadelphia: Fortress, 1977); Tom Holland, *Dominion* (New York City: Basic Books, 2019), 1–17.

3. Hengel, *Crucifixion in the Ancient World*, 55.

4. Perhaps the closest modern parallel to crucifixion is lynching. James Cone observes that Christ's enemies killed him "by hanging him on a tree" (Acts 10:39), and he discusses the similarities between lynching and crucifixion: "Both the cross and the lynching tree were symbols of terror, instruments of torture and execution, reserved primarily for slaves, criminals, and insurrectionists—the lowest of the low in society." James Cone, *The Cross and the Lynching Tree* (Maryknoll, NY: Orbis, 2013), 31. Such a comparison highlights the scandalous nature of the cross and the shame endured by Jesus.

the Greeks) sought salvation through philosophy and wisdom. The thought of a king being crucified was foolishness to them, something only a madman would believe. The picture of the good life was a contemplative philosopher, not a dying criminal.

The mainstream view after the crucifixion was that Jesus was a failure, his followers were fools, and the cross was a defeat. That is certainly what an early graffiti drawing reveals about the way Romans thought about Christians. The drawing depicts a worshiper looking up at Christ dying on the cross. However, in place of Christ's head is the head of a donkey. Below the drawing reads the Greek inscription, "Alexamenos worships his God" (see figure 1). This second-century graffiti represents the foolishness of a gospel proclaiming a crucified Messiah.[5]

Figure 1   Tracing of the Alexamenos graffito.

5. The graffiti was discovered in a building in Rome annexed to the imperial palace on the Palatine. It is now displayed in the Palatine Museum. An image of the graffiti can be viewed at "Scratched Graffito with Blasphemous Crucifix," Palatine Museum, Parco archeologico del Colosseo, https://parcocolosseo.it/en/opere/scratched-graffito -with-blasphemous-crucifix/.

While early Christians were mocked for their belief in the cross, Christians today have often domesticated the cross to make it more palatable for a modern society. Whether placed on a calendar in a Christian bookstore, tattooed on an arm, or elevated above a city skyline, we have tamed the cross and turned it into a decorative pleasantry. But only when we see the horror of the cross will we be ready to understand the glory of the cross.

The Glory of Christ Crucified

When Jesus was crucified, it appeared that his mission had been brought to a devastating halt. From an earthly perspective, the cross was weakness and foolishness. But through the lens of faith, the glory of God shines from the cross like a thousand suns compared to the candle of this world's glory. The love of God through the cross of Christ subverts the wisdom and power of this world, revealing a kingdom that is different than people would expect but greater than they could imagine. The cross is not weakness but rather power controlled by love. The death of Jesus is not foolishness but rather God's wise way of saving the unjust while upholding his justice. This is the awful beauty of the cross.

Herein lies the paradox of the gospel. The self-giving love of God transformed an instrument of death into an instrument of life. The cross is the great reversal, where exaltation comes through humiliation, glory is revealed in shame, victory is accomplished through surrender, and the triumph of the kingdom comes through the suffering of the servant. As Lesslie Newbigin says, "The reign of God has indeed come upon us, and its sign is not a golden throne but a wooden cross."[6] The cross is *good* news because it is God's way of rescuing sinners and restoring the world.

---

6. Lesslie Newbigin, *Foolishness to the Greeks: The Gospel and Western Culture* (Grand Rapids, MI: Eerdmans, 1986), 127.

Faith Seeking Understanding: The Doctrine of Atonement

The doctrine of atonement is the church's attempt to understand the glory of Christ crucified in a way that cultivates worship and catalyzes discipleship. This is what theology is about: faith seeking understanding in service of faithful living. What does it mean that Jesus died "for our sins" (1 Cor. 15:3)? How did his death two millennia ago shape the trajectory of eternity? How does the crucifixion of Christ reveal the wisdom and power of God? The doctrine of atonement seeks to answer these questions not only for our heads but also for our hearts and lives.

Unfortunately, many churches today have exchanged biblical doctrine for pop psychology and costly discipleship for do-it-yourself spirituality. We need a recovery of "sound doctrine, in accordance with the gospel" (1 Tim. 1:10–11) that we might be "transformed by the renewal of [our] minds" (Rom. 12:2). And where better to start than the doctrine of atonement, which is the "heart of the gospel"[7] and "the Holy of Holies of Christian theology"?[8]

Theology is first and foremost about helping the church pray, worship, and live faithfully to the glory of God. Only in a secondary (and derivative) way does theology confront heresies and contemporary challenges. The primary goal of the doctrine of the atonement is for the church to understand more of the depths of the gospel in order to worship the triune God and live according to his gospel. The goal of this book, therefore, is not intellectual mastery but whole-life discipleship, bringing us to the foot of the cross in worship.

---

7. Kevin Vanhoozer, "Atonement," in *Mapping Modern Theology: A Thematic and Historical Introduction*, ed. Kelly Kapic and Bruce McCormack (Grand Rapids, MI: Baker Academic, 2012), 176.

8. Robert Culpepper, *Interpreting the Atonement* (Grand Rapids, MI: Eerdmans, 1966), 11.

Traditionally, the doctrine of atonement addresses how God has reconciled sinners to himself through Christ's death on the cross. Christ deals with sin in a way that takes what is torn asunder and makes it one again. In other words, his death brings about "at-one-ment" between God and sinners. I uphold this approach but expand it in two ways.

First, the scope of Christ's atoning work must be broadened beyond humanity to the whole creation. As Colossians 1:19–20 says, "For in him all the fullness of God was pleased to dwell, and through him to reconcile to himself all things, whether on earth or in heaven, making peace by the blood of his cross." Christ's work on the cross brings about "at-one-ment" with God and sinners within a broader story of the "at-one-ment" of heaven and earth.

Second, the cross is central but must not be solo in the doctrine of atonement. The centrality of the cross is evident from the preeminence of the passion narratives in the Gospels and its prominence throughout the rest of Scripture, casting a shadow backwards over the entire Old Testament and giving vision forward for the church in the New Testament. From the bruised heel of Genesis 3:15 to the slain Lamb of Revelation 5:6, the Bible is the story of a crucified Messiah bringing God's reign on earth as it is in heaven. The apostle Paul summarizes his entire message with the words "Christ crucified" (1 Cor. 1:23). For these reasons, Athanasius is right to say that the cross "is the very center of our faith."[9] The cross is the climax of the Christian story and the center of Christian theology.

To call the cross *central* does not mean that it is the *only* moment of the atonement but rather the most definitive. When Paul summarized the Christian message as "Christ crucified" (1 Cor. 1:23), he was not dismissing the importance of the in-

---

9. Athanasius, *On the Incarnation*, trans. and ed. a Religious of C.S.M.V. (Crestwood, NY: St. Vladimir's Seminary Press, 2002), 48 (4.19).

carnation or resurrection (as is evident from the rest of 1 Corinthians). The cross is the center that represents the whole of the Christian faith.[10]

Figure 2   The cross is central but must be understood within the comprehensive work of Christ.

The various aspects of Christ's ministry ought not compete but rather complement one another in Christ's kingdom mission. Fleming Rutledge playfully compares the death and resurrection of Jesus to a ham and cheese sandwich: "If you're making a ham and cheese sandwich, you don't ask which is more important, the ham or the cheese. If you don't have both of them it isn't a ham and cheese sandwich. Moving from the ridiculous to the sublime, you can't have the crucifixion without the resurrection—and vice versa."[11] The same is true for the whole of Christ's work. If you lose the incarnation, life, ministry, death, resurrection, ascension, or return of Christ, then you lose the gospel.

The focus should be on understanding the particular role of each aspect of Christ's work and discovering how these aspects fit together as a whole. The incarnation, life, death, resurrection, ascension, and return of Christ form a single entity, ultimately finding coherence in the Son himself who is sent by the Father and anointed by the Spirit.

To summarize: *The doctrine of atonement is the church's faith seeking understanding of the way in which Christ, through*

---

10. These elements will be unpacked especially in chapter 2. It is worth noting here that "resurrection" in this visual also entails the ascension and session of Christ.

11. Fleming Rutledge, *The Crucifixion: Understanding the Death of Jesus Christ* (Grand Rapids, MI: Eerdmans, 2015), 64.

all of his work but primarily his death, has dealt with sin and its effects to reconcile sinners and renew creation.

The Approach of This Book

We must avoid two pitfalls that plague atonement theology today. On the one hand, there is the error of one-dimensional reductionism, which focuses on one aspect or theory of the atonement to the exclusion of all others—as if Christ *either* bore our punishment *or* conquered evil *or* demonstrated his love as an example. But to reduce Christ's atoning work to one aspect is to truncate the gospel and diminish God's glory in salvation.

On the other hand, the common reaction to one-dimensional reductionism that we must also avoid is disconnected plurality. This approach celebrates the many dimensions of Christ's atoning work but lacks integration and balance, resulting in a smorgasbord approach based on preference or context. Although contextualization is essential with the atonement, the dimensions of Christ's work are not alternative options but rather overlapping aspects of a comprehensive work.

One-Dimensional Reductionism   Disconnected Plurality

Figure 3   Atonement theology must avoid the opposite errors of one-dimensional reductionism and disconnected plurality.

Here is my approach to the atonement in a nutshell: The death of Christ is a multidimensional accomplishment within the story that begins in the garden and culminates in the kingdom. While the achievements of the cross (forgiveness, victory, adoption, and so on) are unending, the heart of the cross, out of which everything flows and finds its coherence, is Christ dying in our place for our sins. The atoning work of Christ not only reconciles sinners to God but also to one another, calling us into a life of taking up our crosses as we follow our King. In other words, we need a kingdom-framed, substitution-centered, multidimensional, integrated, communal, life-changing approach to the doctrine of atonement.[12]

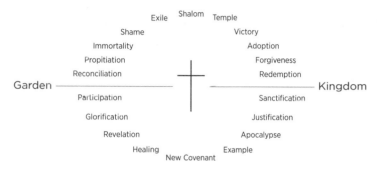

Figure 4   The atonement is a multidimensional accomplishment.

Triune Atonement

From beginning to end, Christ's atoning work is thoroughly Trinitarian. While the doctrine of atonement focuses on Jesus, one must remember that Jesus is the Son of the Father who is empowered by the Spirit to accomplish the triune mission of redemption. Jesus is "the image of the invisible God" (Col. 1:15) and "the exact imprint of his nature" (Heb. 1:3). Therefore, we must affirm the principle of inseparable operations—that is, that the external works of the Trinity are undivided (*opera*

---

12. I find "theories" to be an unhelpful approach to the doctrine of atonement and prefer instead to focus on the many dimensions of the atonement. "Theory" language was not used in the doctrine of atonement until the 1850s as the Enlightenment influenced theological method and theologians sought to find their place in the modern university system. Adam Johnson demonstrates how "theories" impose a scientific structure from the Enlightenment on God's revelation in Scripture. Furthermore, he argues that it is anachronistic to use "theory" language for the history of the doctrine, as if, for example, Irenaeus was presenting a "theory" of recapitulation. See Adam J. Johnson, "Theories and *Theoria* of the Atonement: A Proposal," *International Journal of Systematic Theology* 23, no. 1 (March 2021): 92–108.

trinitatis ad extra sunt indivisa). As Gregory of Nyssa says, "Every operation which extends from God to creation . . . has its origin from the Father, and proceeds through the Son, and is perfected in the Holy Spirit."[13]

Many theories of atonement have gone awry because they are insufficiently Trinitarian, often pitting the Father against the Son and leaving out the Holy Spirit altogether.[14] Yet Scripture is clear: God's kingdom mission, with atonement at the heart of it, is a unified work of the Father, Son, and Holy Spirit (John 7:39; 2 Cor. 5:19; Gal. 1:4; Col. 1:19–20; Heb. 9:14). The doctrine of atonement unravels without the doctrine of the Trinity. As Hans Urs von Balthasar says, "The events of the cross can only be interpreted against the background of the Trinity."[15]

A Multigenerational, Multicultural Approach

To learn about the doctrine of atonement is to join a conversation among the saints who have been led by the Holy Spirit in understanding the depths of the cross from generation to generation. While I have been shaped by many different traditions, the greatest influences on my understanding of the atonement are the North African church father Athanasius, the Dutch theologian Herman Bavinck, and the English pastor theologian John Stott.[16] My hope is that this book reflects

---

13. Gregory of Nyssa, "On 'Not Three Gods,'" in *Dogmatic Treatises*, in vol. 5 of *Nicene and Post-Nicene Fathers*, Series 2, ed. Philip Schaff and Henry Wace (New York: Cosimo Classics, n.d.), 334.

14. Many of the critiques regarding divine violence and "cosmic child abuse" are in response to theories of atonement that are not sufficiently Trinitarian. While not having space in this brief volume to engage those critiques, I hope to provide an account of the atonement that does not fall prey to them.

15. Hans Urs von Balthasar, *The Action*, vol. 4 of *Theo-Drama: Theological Dramatic Theory*, trans. Graham Harrison (San Francisco: Ignatius, 1994), 319.

16. See Athanasius, *On the Incarnation*; Herman Bavinck, *Sin and Salvation in Christ*, vol. 3 of *Reformed Dogmatics*, ed. John Bolt, trans. John Vriend (Grand Rapids, MI: Baker Academic, 2003); John Stott, *The Cross of Christ* (Downers Grove, IL: InterVarsity Press, 1986).

their collective influence. Furthermore, since the atonement is a global accomplishment, it will be best understood from a global perspective. For this reason, I have sought to interact with majority world scholars throughout my research and writing and have benefited greatly from these brothers and sisters throughout the world.[17]

The Secular Longing for Atonement

Our sin-ridden world is longing for atonement. Do not let secularism make you think that we have evolved beyond such a need. As Charles Taylor argues, secularism is not the absence of religious belief but rather a whole new set of beliefs, redirecting our deepest longings onto something other than God.[18] While we have attempted to suppress our longing for atonement, it keeps pushing through, even if in different, less traditional ways. For example, the innate longing for atonement can be seen in popular article titles, such as "Anger and Atonement during a Pandemic" and "Spain's Attempt to Atone for a 500-Year-Old Sin."[19] *The New York Times* revealed their "Word of the Day" for May 16, 2011, as "atone," and the newspaper noted that forty-three of its articles over the previous year had talked about atonement.[20] As another example, consider the advice of a New Age guru: "The only way to atone for the past is to do something meaningful in the present."[21]

---

17. For a helpful introduction to global theology, see Timothy C. Tennent, *Theology in the Context of World Christianity: How the Global Church Is Influencing the Way We Think About and Discuss Theology* (Grand Rapids, MI: Zondervan Academic, 2007).

18. See Charles Taylor, *A Secular Age* (Cambridge, MA: Belknap, 2007).

19. Daniel W. Drezner, "Anger and Atonement during a Pandemic," *Washington Post*, September 30, 2020, https://www.washingtonpost.com/; Kiku Adatto, "Spain's Attempt to Atone for a 500-Year-Old Sin," *The Atlantic*, September 21, 2019, https://www.theatlantic.com/.

20. "Word of the Day: Atone," *The New York Times*, May 16, 2011, https://archive.nytimes.com/learning.blogs.nytimes.com/2011/05/16/word-of-the-day-atone.

21. This quote is commonly attributed to Deepak Chopra, although the original source is unknown.

Our society is aching for atonement. How can we deal with our guilt and shame? How can we be set free from our past? How can all that is wrong be made right? The assumption in these questions is that *we* can atone for our sins. But the message of Christianity is not about what we ought to do for God but what God has done for us. The good news is that God has sent his Son, empowered by the Spirit, to atone for our sins and make right all that our sin has made wrong. And the gospel goes far beyond merely "making amends" (which is how the word "atonement" is often used today). Through the sacrificial death of Christ, forgiveness, freedom, healing, and restoration are available not only for broken people but for all of creation. This is good news.

1

The Story of Atonement

From a Garden to a Kingdom

*The time is fulfilled, and the kingdom of God
is at hand; repent and believe in the gospel.*
MARK 1:15

*The cross, standing between creation and final
consummation, is not an accident. . . . It is,
on the contrary, the supreme instance of the
manner in which God's power operates.*[1]
JUSTO L. GONZALEZ

My wife looked at me, scissors in hand, and said, "I'm going to
cut off your head." Based on this statement alone, you might
assume that my wife is a bloodthirsty maniac who was about
to decapitate her husband. She's not. She is kind, loving, and

---

1. Justo L. González, *Mañana: Christian Theology from a Hispanic Perspective*
(Nashville: Abingdon, 1990), 93.

godly. But you wouldn't know that because a statement derives its meaning from the broader story of which it is a part. Here is the story: My wife was scrapbooking and needed a picture of our daughter by herself. When she could only find a picture with me in it, she looked at me with an I-love-you-but-I-have-to-do-this look, and said, "I'm going to cut off your head."

My point is simple and equally applies to the doctrine of atonement: the story or context in which a statement or event occurs reveals its meaning. What, then, is the meaning of the statement "Christ died for our sins"? We must have the right story.[2]

The Wrong Story

Many end up with the wrong doctrine of atonement because they have the wrong story or framework. Let's look at a few common examples of unhelpful frameworks before going to the Scriptures for the right one.

Going to Heaven When You Die

I went to church camp in junior high and heard a common gospel presentation: "You're a sinner and are going to hell. But while your sin has made a great chasm between you and God, the cross bridges the chasm so you can come to God. Christ died for your sins so that you can go to heaven when you die."

There is much to be commended in this story—namely, the reality of sin and the cross as God's solution. However, while the individual elements of the story are true, the way they are put together (and what they leave out) leads to a devastatingly unbiblical narrative. There are at least five ways this story falls

---

2. Kevin Vanhoozer rightly warns of the temptation "to regard narrative simply as the pretty packaging of historical content to be torn off and discarded." Kevin Vanhoozer, *The Drama of Doctrine: A Canonical-Linguistic Approach to Christian Theology* (Louisville: Westminster John Knox, 2005), 282. Theology arises from narrative. But narrative is not merely a vessel for theological content but rather shapes the content and is part of the content itself.

short. First, this is a "sin and salvation" story that culminates in a disembodied existence. The biblical story, however, bookends sin and salvation with creation and new creation. The final goal is not an immaterial heaven but a renewed creation. The story of the Bible is not about leaving earth for heaven but rather the kingdom of heaven coming on earth. Second, this story is thoroughly individualistic, focusing solely on "me and God." This is a far cry from the biblical story of God redeeming a people to create a new family. Third, this is ultimately a story of how we can come to God, whereas Scripture is primarily a story of how God has come to us. Fourth, this story works apart from the Trinity, which makes it not distinctly Christian. Fifth, there is no place or need for Israel and the Old Testament in this story. So while there are truths in the story, the story itself is incomplete, resulting in a me-centered, over-spiritualized, non-Trinitarian view of the cross. This "gospel presentation" has been shaped as much by Greek Gnosticism and Western individualism as by the story of Scripture.

Making the World a Better Place

In the seventeenth century a new story began to emerge in the Western world. We are no longer in the Dark Ages of religious superstition and fairytales but have been enlightened by modern science, technology, and humanity's potential to bring the world to its appointed end. How does this story of human progress shed light on the cross?

Nineteenth-century German theologians sought to answer this question, and their work greatly influenced American pastors such as Walter Rauschenbusch in New York City. Subscribing to the enlightenment narrative while trying to maintain Christian identity within it, Rauschenbusch rejected substitutionary atonement (along with the bodily resurrection of Christ and the inspiration of the Scriptures) and redefined the gospel in terms of what we do to care for the marginalized.[3]

While there are elements of truth in the social gospel movement (especially its emphasis on God's heart for the poor and marginalized), it is a cautionary tale of Christian morals being hijacked by an unbiblical narrative. In this story, the cross is often ignored entirely or at best is reduced to an example of identifying with the broken. The emphasis is not on what Christ has done for us but on how we can make the world a better place.

The American Dream

A temptation for many cultures is not merely to reject the gospel but to enlist it as a way of achieving greater cultural goals. In the United States (and beyond) the greater goal is the American Dream, with its suburban vision of 2.3 kids and a well-manicured lawn, or the urban version of casting off the oppressive structures of society and discovering yourself. In either case, the master narrative is one of individual happiness, and the gospel becomes another way of rounding out the spiritual side of an otherwise holistic self-improvement project.

This approach also has elements of truth, particularly the God-given good of family and the individual rights that come with human dignity. The narrative, however, reflects late modernity (a reaction against enlightenment metanarratives), which rejects the idea of truth altogether and encourages individuals to create their own personal vision of flourishing. Within this framework, the cross becomes a key that unlocks your potential, helping you become your best self and achieve your dreams. Self-fulfilment supplants self-denial and the cross becomes another instrument for building our personal kingdoms.

---

3. Walter Rauschenbusch, *A Theology for the Social Gospel* (New York: Macmillan, 1917); see esp. chap. 19, "The Social Gospel and the Atonement."

Looking for the Right Story

We have seen thus far that the meaning of the cross is determined by the narrative within which it is understood. The wrong story leads to the wrong doctrine of atonement. Christians believe that the one true story of the world is the story of Scripture. When Paul discussed the meaning of Christ's death with the church in Corinth, he said that Christ died for our sins "in accordance with the Scriptures" (1 Cor. 15:3–4). This does not merely mean that the suffering of the Messiah fulfilled a few prophecies here and there but that it is the climactic fulfilment of the whole story. The grand narrative of Scripture must be the framework for how we understand what took place at Golgotha.

How, then, can we summarize the story of Scripture? While there are many ways, let's take our lead from the opening words of Jesus's ministry: "The time is fulfilled, and the kingdom of God is at hand; repent and believe in the gospel" (Mark 1:15). The Bible is the story of the kingdom of God.[4] So how does the kingdom story bring meaning and coherence to Christ's death on the cross? Before answering that question, I will provide a concise definition of the kingdom of God and then share several reasons why it is a helpful framework for atonement.

The Kingdom of God

The kingdom of God is a vast, expansive idea—not the kind of thing to yawn over. But I will offer a concise working definition in eight words: The kingdom is *God's reign through God's people over God's place.*

---

4. The theme of the kingdom is paramount in the Old Testament, especially in Psalms and Isaiah, which deeply shape the New Testament. The kingdom of God is the number one thing Jesus talked about, and Paul's teaching is summarized as testifying to the kingdom of God (Acts 28:23, 31). For a further exploration of the theme of the kingdom of God, see Jeremy Treat, *Seek First: How the Kingdom of God Changes Everything* (Grand Rapids, MI: Zondervan, 2019).

God's Reign

Far too often when people talk about the kingdom, they speak of something akin to a kingdom without a king. But the kingdom is first and foremost about God. God is King! God reigns! In fact, the phrase "kingdom of God" in Greek could also be translated as the "kingship of God." The vision of the kingdom is not a utopian dream but rather a vision of the world re-ordered around God's royal grace.

God's People

God reigns over his people, and he reigns through his people. We are, after all, made in his image, meant to reflect his compassionate rule. Sin, however, fractured humanity's relationship with God and corrupted the goodness of God's creation. But God did not give up on his kingdom project. God will reclaim his reign over all of creation, and at the heart of the coming of the kingdom is the reconciliation of the King's people.

God's Place

The kingdom is a vision of God's reign *on earth* as it is in heaven. It began in a garden. But the garden kingdom was meant to become a global kingdom, where people from every tribe and tongue flourish under the merciful kingship of God. And while the idea of saving souls is correct, it is not complete. God is a great King who has promised to renew all things (Rev. 21:5).

Jesus and the Kingdom

All the promises of the kingdom are fulfilled in Christ. *God's reign* is embodied in Christ. *God's people* are those who are in Christ. *God's place* of a renewed creation begins with the resurrected body of Christ. Jesus is Israel's Messiah—the anointed King—who came to establish God's kingdom. And yet, Christ brings the kingdom in a way that subverts the world's expectations and yet fulfils humanity's deepest desires. In this kingdom, the throne is a cross, and the King reigns with mercy and grace.

Why the Kingdom Is a Helpful Framework

Aside from the fact that the kingdom is one of the primary ways of telling the metanarrative of Scripture, there are four reasons why it serves as a helpful framework for the doctrine of atonement.

Grounded in the Old Testament

Framing the atonement with the kingdom story grounds Christ's work in the story of Israel and highlights his identity as the seed of Abraham and the Son of David. Jesus is not a generic superhero but is rather the Jewish Messiah who came to fulfill God's Old Testament promises. Furthermore, New Testament language regarding atonement is meaningless apart from its Old Testament background. "Redemption" is rooted in the exodus, "sacrifice" is grounded in the Levitical system, and so on. A doctrine of atonement not anchored in the Old Testament will drift into a meaning far from the story of Scripture.

Connected to Community

The concept of a kingdom is intrinsically communal and, therefore, undercuts the temptation to develop a doctrine of atonement in light of an individualistic, privatized spirituality. Christ's atoning work is aimed at a covenant people who are ransomed into the kingdom of God.

Embracing Comprehensive Salvation

Atonement theology, especially at the popular level, has been plagued by reductionism. Whether limiting Christ's work to a purely spiritual salvation or only focusing on one of the dimensions of his work, many have truncated the breadth of Christ's atoning death. A kingdom framework gives a comprehensive view of salvation, encompassing the renewal of heaven and earth while embracing the many dimensions of the atonement.

Tethered to Discipleship

After Jesus began his ministry by proclaiming the arrival of the kingdom of God, he immediately called his first disciples to himself (Mark 1:14–17). The proclamation of the kingdom includes the call to follow the King (discipleship). This prevents our atonement theology from slipping into impractical theorizing and calls us to follow the crucified Messiah.

The Story of the Kingdom

The kingdom of God is the master narrative that gives meaning to the cross. It is a comprehensive vision (God's reign over all of creation) with a core focus (God's covenant relationship with his people). The cross is the climax of a story that begins in the garden and culminates in a kingdom. We will now look at that story, divided into five chapters: the garden kingdom, the rival kingdom, the promised kingdom, the cross-shaped kingdom, and the eternal kingdom.

The Garden Kingdom

The story begins in a garden. Although the phrase "kingdom of God" does not come until later, the concept of the kingdom has its roots in the soil of Eden. God is presented in the creation narrative as a King who reigns through his word. He speaks, and it is so. But he is not like the earthly kings we have become accustomed to throughout world history. He reigns with love. He uses his power to bless. He delights in his creation. And after declaring everything he created "good," God makes humanity and exclaims, "Very good" (Gen. 1:31). The apex of the King's creation is not majestic mountains or awe-inspiring oceans but rather man and woman together before God.

Adam and Eve are made in the image of God (Gen. 1:27), which means not only that they reflect God and, therefore, have intrinsic dignity and value but also that they are meant to represent God's rule on earth. This begins in the garden of Eden, where God places Adam and Eve to enjoy the goodness of his creation. However, not only did God give them an invitation to delight, he also gave them a mandate to "work" and "keep" the garden (Gen. 2:15). But contrary to popular opinion, Adam and Eve were not meant to stay in the garden. They were called to "fill the earth and subdue it" (Gen. 1:28). This is royal language. God is King, but he reigns through his image-bearing people. The command to subdue does not mean to exploit the earth—quite the opposite. It means to responsibly steward and care for the King's creation.

Eden, therefore, is the starting point. While Eden was a beautifully ordered garden, the rest of the world was wild and untamed. God's creation was good, but it was made with potential built into it. Adam and Eve were called by God to go from the garden and cultivate the earth, making it more like Eden. In other words, they were to Edenize the world. God's creation in Genesis 1–2 was not a final product but rather an unfinished project—a kingdom project.[5]

---

5. Psalm 8 interprets Gen. 1 in this way, recounting how in creation God crowned humanity with glory and honor and gave them dominion over the earth.

Genesis 1–2 presents a comprehensive view of the purpose of the world where God reigns, humanity thrives, and all of creation reflects the glory of God. At the heart of this comprehensive vision is the relational union of God and his people, as well as the cosmic union between heaven (the dwelling place of God) and earth (the dwelling place of humanity). Eden offers a vision of heaven on earth, God dwelling with his people.[6]

How does the creation portion of the story affect our understanding of the atonement? It is immensely important yet often overlooked. The Bible is a story that begins with creation and ends with new creation, and in the center is the King on the cross, making all things new. To say that the cross is at the center is not merely a statement of its utmost importance but also of its place. The crucifixion of the Messiah gains its meaning from that which comes before and after it.

So while we begin with Christ crucified as the supreme revelation of God, a solution (the doctrine of atonement) assumes a problem (the doctrine of sin), which presupposes an original purpose (the doctrine of creation). Creation reveals God's purpose of establishing his kingdom over all the earth, and this must shape the very mission for which Christ came.

Athanasius begins *On the Incarnation* by discussing the significance of creation for salvation.

> We will begin, then, with the creation of the world and with God its Maker, for the first fact that you must grasp is this: the renewal of creation has been wrought by the Self-same Word Who made it in the beginning. There is thus no incon-

---

6. Adam's task to "work" and "keep" (Gen. 2:15) the garden is the same role—and is described with the same words—as the role assigned to the priests in the temple (Num. 3:7–8; 8:26; 18:5–6). This is a clue to a deep meaning embedded in the creation narrative. Eden is like a temple where heaven (the dwelling place of God) and earth (the dwelling place of man) come together. Adam is a priest-king called to rule by serving in the Edenic temple.

sistency between creation and salvation; for the One Father
has employed the same Agent for both works, effecting the
salvation of the world through the same Word Who made
it in the beginning.[7]

Just as the world was created by the Father through the Son
in the power of the Spirit, the world will be recreated by the
Father through the Son in the power of the Spirit. Salvation,
therefore, is the restoration of creation. The goal is not merely
to get back to Eden but rather to recover the vision of Eden:
the kingdom of God.

If a doctrine of atonement skips over creation and begins
with the fall, then it will miss the scope of God's original intent
and likely end up with a gnostic view of salvation that extracts
the spiritual elements of what is meant to be a comprehensive,
enmeshed world. The atonement is about the reconciliation of
all things (Col. 1:20).

The Rival Kingdom

Instead of representing God's rule over creation, Adam and Eve
submit to the rule of one of God's creatures, the serpent. This
sin not only separates fallen humanity from God but also de-
rails God's calling on humanity to extend God's gracious reign
throughout the earth. Rather than spreading the blessings of
God's kingdom, they are exiled from the garden, which leads
instead to spreading the curse of sin.

The gravity of humanity's sin cannot be overstated. God's
diagnosis in Genesis 6 was that "the wickedness of man was
great in the earth" and that their hearts were "only evil continually" (Gen. 6:5; cf. Ps. 14:3). Herman Bavinck captures the
severity of sin in the story of Scripture: "Sin ruined the entire

---

7. Athanasius, *On the Incarnation*, trans. and ed. a Religious of C.S.M.V. (Crestwood, NY: St. Vladimir's Seminary Press, 2002), 26 (1.1).

creation, converting its righteousness into guilt, its holiness into impurity, its glory into shame, its blessedness into misery, its harmony into disorder, and its light into darkness."[8]

Sin is a multidimensional problem within the story of God establishing his loving rule over all creation. Since sin is the problem for which Christ's atoning work is the solution, we must have a biblical and comprehensive grasp of its nature. Three questions need to be answered:

- What is sin?
- What is the primary impact of sin?
- What are the multidimensional effects of sin?

First, what is sin? The most common Greek word for sin (*harmatia*) means "to miss the mark." As we have seen, the mark—God's intended purpose for humanity—is to know him and represent his loving rule throughout the earth. Sin, therefore, is not merely a mistake or a moral flaw. Sin is a personal rejection of God as King and a relinquishing of the responsibility that humanity was given to rule over the earth on God's behalf. While humanity was made to live for God's kingdom and to glorify his name, sin is our attempt to build our own kingdoms and make a name for ourselves.

The rejection of God as King always comes with the attempt to replace him with something else on the throne. The Bible often speaks of this replacement with the language of idolatry. An idol is anything we look to in place of God for our identity, security, and satisfaction. Sin, therefore, is not merely doing bad things but is also making good things into ultimate things. And while people often assume that idolatry only applies to ancient people kneeling before handmade gods, it is just as prevalent in

---

8. Herman Bavinck, *Sin and Salvation in Christ*, vol. 3 of *Reformed Dogmatics*, ed. John Bolt, trans. John Vriend (Grand Rapids, MI: Baker Academic, 2003), 29.

our culture today. Modern people worship the idols of money, sex, power, career, and reputation.

Yet, if I am the one who chooses the idols I serve and who decides what is right and wrong, then the ultimate object of my worship and devotion is not the idols of money, sex, or power—it's me. Sin is our attempt to dethrone God and enthrone ourselves. The word *autonomy*, which represents one of the highest values in our culture today, means "self-rule." Sin is substitution—the attempt to replace the divine King with the sovereign self so that individual desire reigns, personal choice is the authority, and freedom is defined by independence.

Second, what is the primary impact of sin? The answer in the narrative of Genesis 3 (banishment from the presence of God) is reaffirmed throughout Scripture: the primary impact of sin is the separation of God and humanity (Isa. 59:2). In place of intimacy, unity, and life is now hostility, division, and death. Humanity, created to delight in the love of Father, Son, and Holy Spirit, is alienated from God and under his righteous judgment (Rom. 2:1–5).

This sin-induced separation, however, is not restricted to the divine-human relationship. Immediately after humanity is cut off from God in Genesis 3, we learn in Genesis 4 of the violent opposition of brother against brother. Furthermore, because of human sin, heaven and earth have been torn asunder. In all, sin brings separation between God and humanity, division among people, and the rupture of heaven and earth.

Third, what are the multidimensional effects of sin? Sin brings in its wake disaster in many forms, revealing what African theologian John Pobee calls the "many-sidedness of sin."[9] It is imperative to recognize the multidimensional nature of sin, for a narrow view of sin will lead to a narrow doctrine of

---

9. John Pobee, *Toward an African Theology* (Nashville: Abingdon, 1979), 107.

atonement. Acknowledging the complex and integrated nature of sin, however, will lead to a complex and integrated understanding of Christ's atoning work.

Because of sin against God, people are

- unable to see the glory of God (2 Cor. 4:4);
- enemies of God (James 4:4);
- deserving of God's judgment (Rom. 1:18);
- under the sway of the devil (Eph. 2:2);
- enslaved to sin (John 8:34);
- condemned (Rom. 5:16);
- stained morally (Zech. 3:3);
- covered in shame (Jer. 17:13);
- bound to the law (Rom. 7:6);
- ignorant of the truth (Rom. 1:18);
- exiled (2 Kings 17:6–7);
- spiritual orphans (Rom. 8:15);
- part of the evil age (Gal. 1:4);
- physically ill (Mark 2:3–12);
- far from God (Eph. 2:13);
- in need of an example (Matt. 5:14);
- spiritually indebted (Col. 2:14);
- alienated from the life of God (Eph. 4:18);
- dead in transgressions (Eph. 2:1);
- hostile to God and others (Rom. 8:7).

The effects of sin do not remain disconnected from one another as if the result of unrelated destructive forces. Rather, the cumulative effects of sin come together under the sway of an evil power to form a sinful kingdom in opposition to God. The devil is a pretender king who rules with deception, temptation, and accusation. Humanity, made to flourish under God's rule, has voluntarily chosen to enlist in the kingdom of darkness and is now under the influence of the world, the flesh, and the devil. The irony is that in all our attempts to rule ourselves and build our own kingdoms, we end up submitting to the rule of another, the serpent king who deceived our parents in Eden. The deception of autonomy was his plan all along: to allure us with self-rule so that in thinking we run our own lives, we increase in our rebellion against the good and holy King.

How does the doctrine of sin shape the doctrine of atonement? First, we must properly diagnose the problem (sin) in order to rightly understand the solution (atonement). Second, sin is first and foremost against God but is multidimensional in its effects. We should, therefore, expect a doctrine of atonement that reconciles God and humanity *and* deals with the various effects of sin. Furthermore, a significant implication of a thorough doctrine of sin is that the death of Christ is *necessary* for God to deal with sin and restore his purposes for creation. This is a true litmus test for various doctrines of atonement. Is the death of Jesus absolutely necessary to deal with sin, or is it merely a gesture on behalf of humanity in need of help?

The Promised Kingdom

The sin of humanity is grave, but it cannot thwart God's purposes. In response to rebellion in the garden, God promises that the seed of a woman will crush the serpent while being wounded in the process (Gen. 3:15). This serpent-crushing King will reverse the curse, reconcile God and sinners, and realize God's original purpose of establishing his kingdom over all the earth. However, while the royal vision remains, the kingdom will come into a fallen world through surprisingly different means. A pattern emerges from this point onward whereby victory comes through suffering, exaltation through humiliation, and ultimately the kingdom through the cross.

The rest of the Bible is the story of God keeping this promise of a sacrificial, serpent-crushing King. Through the unfolding plot of the Old Testament, we begin to see how the ruin of humanity's sin will be overcome by the reign of humanity's Savior. The light that would one day shine on the cross of Christ casts a shadow all the way back to this great promise.

The story unfolds in the Old Testament, showing that God's kingdom comes in the most counterintuitive ways: humility, service, and sacrifice. God promises Abraham that he will reverse the curse and bless all the families of the earth, and then he symbolically commits to bearing the covenant curse himself (Gen. 15:17–21; cf. Jer. 34:18). Joseph's ascension to royalty is characterized by suffering, and he exercises his reign over his brothers with forgiveness. In the exodus, God sets his people free *from* slavery and *for* his kingdom through the means of a sacrificial lamb (Ex. 12). The book of Ruth reveals how God uses an overlooked outsider to bring redemption to his people. David's royalty is characterized by righteous suffering (Ps. 22), and he conquers an evil giant through humble means (1 Sam. 17). Zechariah tells of a humble king who will reign over creation and redeem his people with the blood of his covenant (Zech. 9:9–12).

The book of Isaiah is the apex of the Old Testament's revelation of how the kingdom will come in a counterintuitive way. Isaiah 52:7–12 announces the good news of God's reign and how the divine King will bring about a new exodus, delivering his people from bondage and redeeming them into his kingdom. But how will the kingdom come? "Behold, my servant" begins the song recorded in Isaiah 52:13–53:12. The victory of the kingdom comes through the suffering of the servant. By bearing the sins of his people, the servant will bring about a new exodus and establish God's reign.

The kingdom vision of Israel was majestic and lofty, but the Old Testament ends modestly with only partial fulfilment, far from anything like a King ushering in a new era of salvation. But the promise remains. The anticipation builds. How will God's kingdom come, and who will be the anointed Messiah?

The Cross-Shaped Kingdom

Jesus began his ministry by announcing that the kingdom of God had arrived and was being fulfilled in him (Mark 1:14–15). He gave sight to the blind. He cast out demons. He healed the sick. He forgave sin. He brought in the outcasts. Could this be the fulfillment of Israel's hope for a Messiah who would restore God's reign on earth? Yes. But Jesus was not only revealing his identity as the Messiah, he was also redefining it.

In the Gospel of Mark, when Jesus is first identified as the Messiah, he immediately reshapes his disciples' expectations by saying that as King, he must suffer (Mark 8:31). On the way to the cross, Jesus predicts his death and resurrection three times, each time revealing more of the nature of God's kingdom and showing how it shapes their lives as disciples. After the third prediction, when Jesus redefines greatness by serving, he says to his disciples, "The Son of Man came not to be served but to serve, and to give his life as a ransom for many" (Mark 10:45). Jesus was bringing together two threads of the Old Testament to create a new tapestry of a crucified Messiah. Like the Son of Man from Daniel 7, Jesus would establish God's everlasting kingdom over all the earth. However, like the servant from Isaiah 53, he would accomplish this through his atoning death in the place of his people. The cross is the crowning achievement of Christ's kingdom mission.

The way Mark tells the story of the crucifixion makes clear that Christ's kingdom mission did not cease at the cross. In order to mock him as a pretender king, the Roman soldiers give Jesus a purple robe, a scepter, and a crown of thorns. Above his head is written "King of the Jews." Yet Mark is showing through irony that the one mocked as king truly is King. The crucifixion is a coronation, where Christ is exalted as the rightful ruler of the world. The cross is a throne from which Christ rules the world with grace.

According to Paul, Christ's death in our place deals with our sins in a way that forgives our trespasses (Eph. 1:7), satisfies God's justice (Rom. 3:21–26), defeats the devil (Col. 2:13–15), demonstrates God's love (Rom. 5:8), and unites heaven and earth (Eph. 1:10). Hebrews 2:5–10 presents Jesus as the last Adam who has restored God's royal design for creation and regained the crown of "glory and honor" (Heb. 2:7) for humanity through his death on the cross. Revelation says that Christ is the King who "has freed us from our sins by his blood and made us a kingdom" (Rev. 1:5–6).

Unfortunately, this deep biblical connection between the kingdom and the cross has frequently been overlooked. In fact, a wedge has often been driven between kingdom and cross, with whole camps rallying around each side: the kingdom crowd advocates for social justice and the cross crowd for personal salvation. But while many feel the need to choose between kingdom and cross, Scripture presents a mutually enriching relationship between the two that emerges in the story of Israel and culminates in Christ the crucified King. The kingdom and the cross are not in competition. Christ brings the kingdom by way of the cross. The cross establishes and shapes the kingdom. To put it simply, the cross and the kingdom are held together by the Christ, who brings God's rule on earth as it is in heaven through his atoning death on the cross.

The death of Christ is the decisive moment, though certainly not the only significant moment in the coming of the kingdom.

The kingdom was present in Jesus's life, proclaimed and embodied in his ministry, established by his death, and inaugurated through his resurrection. The kingdom is being advanced by the Spirit through the church and will be consummated in the second coming.[10]

The Eternal Kingdom

The vision of hope offered in the book of Revelation is grounded in the work of the crucified Messiah. In Revelation 5:5–6, John is told about a Lion, but when he turns, he sees instead a Lamb. The slain Lamb is at the throne being praised with the following song:

> Worthy are you to take the scroll
> > and to open its seals,
> for you were slain, and by your blood you ransomed
> > > people for God
> > from every tribe and language and people and nation,
> and you have made them a kingdom and priests to
> > > our God,
> > and they shall reign on the earth. (Rev. 5:9–10)

This is a glimpse of the eternal kingdom of God. Multitudes of people from every nation have been set free and brought together as one family. These are people who have been washed clean, made new, and are filled with joy as they worship their King. They are God's people. And how did all of this come about? The blood of Jesus. The kingdom of God comes through the blood of the Son of God. Miroslav Volf says, "The world to come is ruled by the one who on the cross took violence upon himself in order to conquer and embrace the enemy."[11]

---

10. In the next chapter, we will look closer at each of the aspects of Christ's work.

11. Miroslav Volf, *Exclusion and Embrace: A Theological Exploration of Identity, Otherness, and Reconciliation* (Nashville: Abingdon, 1996), 300.

Revelation, however, does not end only with the union of God and sinners. The renewing effects of Christ's atoning death reach as far as the effects of the sin to which it is a response. Sin not only separated God and humanity but also rent asunder heaven and earth. Revelation 21 is a picture of the union of heaven and earth, coming together like a bride and groom: "Behold, the dwelling place of God is with man" (Rev. 21:3). The atonement brings about the union of God and sinners within the story of the union of heaven and earth.

This eschatological vision for the future ought to deeply shape the doctrine of atonement. For what reason did Christ come? What was the end goal? The telos was not merely forgiving sin so that humanity could try again within a broken creation. The vision—from the beginning—was the full realization of God's reign on earth as it is in heaven. The cross is set within a story that culminates in God's gracious reign through his reconciled people over a renewed creation.

Living by the Story

In this chapter we have sought to understand the cross within the story of the kingdom of God. It is natural, however, when people hear a story to wonder what their place is in the story. Thankfully, Scripture is clear on our role. Through the blood of Christ, not only have we been ransomed into the kingdom but also made a royal priesthood. As Peter tells the dispersed exiles, "You are a chosen race, a royal priesthood, a holy nation, a people for his own possession, that you may proclaim the excellencies of him who called you out of darkness into his marvelous light" (1 Pet. 2:9).

The identity of a royal priesthood explodes with meaning when understood within the story of the kingdom. Adam was called to be a royal priest in Eden, working and keeping the garden and subduing the earth. When Israel was brought out of slavery from Egypt, God declared to them, "You shall be to me a kingdom of priests" (Ex. 19:6). But where Adam and Israel failed, Jesus perfectly fulfilled the role of a royal priest. And now, those who are in Christ are called to be a royal priesthood, to worship our King and work for his kingdom purposes. By God's grace, we are a people who stand at the intersection of heaven and earth, proclaiming God's gracious rule and embodying the righteousness and justice of his kingdom in our lives.

2

The Heart of Atonement

The Great Exchange

For Christ also suffered once for sins, the righteous for the unrighteous, that he might bring us to God.
1 PETER 3:18

By offering himself as a perfect sacrifice for sin, Jesus opened the way to God, dealing with the fundamental problem of the broken relationship between God and humanity.[1]
SICILY MBURA MURIITHI

The cross is a multidimensional accomplishment within the story of the kingdom of God. To go deeper into the doctrine of atonement, however, we must acknowledge the key distinction

---

1. Sicily Mbura Muriithi, "1 Peter," in *Africa Bible Commentary: A One-Volume Commentary Written by 70 African Scholars*, ed. Tokunboh Adeyemo (Nairobi, Kenya: WordAlive, 2006), 1548.

between *what* Christ accomplished (the outcome) and *how* he accomplished it (the means). A robust doctrine of atonement will include both.[2] Chapter 3 will discuss *what* Christ accomplished: reconciliation, adoption, victory, and many of the other dimensions of the comprehensive vision of the kingdom of God. This chapter will explain the heart of atonement—that is, *how* Christ's life, death, and resurrection accomplished "at-one-ment" between God and sinners, along with the many-splendored outcomes of this glorious accomplishment. In short, the means of atonement is substitution: Christ died in our place for our sins.

Substitution, therefore, is not another dimension of the atonement but rather undergirds all the dimensions of the atonement. As the heart pumps blood throughout the body, the substitutionary work of Christ gives meaning and coherence to every aspect of what God has accomplished through his Son.

In Our Place

The heart of the atonement—the means by which Christ accomplishes his multidimensional work—is that Christ died in our place for our sins. The Messiah took on all the consequences of our rebellion so that we can experience all the blessings of his kingdom. This is the great exchange:

- He died so that we can live.
- He was cursed so that we can be blessed.
- He was wounded so that we can be healed.
- He went into exile so that we can be at home.
- He was crushed so that we can be made whole.

---

2. In my estimation, the early church focused more on the means of atonement while much of contemporary theology has shifted to the outcome of atonement. I agree with Benjamin Myers that unless one addresses how Christ's death brings about atonement, it is an incomplete and insufficient approach. Benjamin Myers, "The Patristic Atonement Model," in *Locating Atonement: Explorations in Constructive Dogmatics*, ed. Oliver Crisp and Fred Sanders (Grand Rapids, MI: Zondervan Academic, 2015), 71.

- He carried our guilt so that we can be forgiven.
- He bore our shame so that we can receive honor.
- He experienced defeat so that we can have victory.
- He was condemned so that we can be declared innocent.
- He took our moral stains so that we can be washed clean.
- He was plunged into darkness so that we can walk in the light.

To say that Christ is our substitute means that he takes our place *and* that we take his. We do not merely receive a blank slate or a fresh start. We are given the righteousness of Christ and the deposit of the Holy Spirit. Far from being a cold transaction, this is a covenantal exchange where orphans are made sons and daughters.[3] The cross is not an exacting commercial negotiation but rather an exchange that creates a superabundant atonement. As John Chrysostom says, "Christ paid off much more than we owed—as much more as a limitless ocean compared to a small drop of water."[4]

How can one man's bloody death on a cross be considered good news? Because he suffered, as the Nicene Creed says, "for us . . . and for our salvation."[5] He took what was ours because of sin and gave us what is his by grace. Jesus lived the life we could not live, died the death we should have died, and rose so that we can have life in him. The King became a servant to bring us into his kingdom. And it all hinges on substitution. As John

---

3. Perhaps, for some, the language of *substitution* may seem a bit cold for the greatest act of love in the history of the world. After all, one can substitute tofu for meat or a right-handed pitcher for a left-handed pitcher. Is this word worthy of describing the Son's death to rescue humanity? Like any theological word (such as *incarnation* or *Trinity*), *substitution* is theological shorthand for a whole web of beliefs, which I will unpack in this chapter and which are beautifully life-giving.

4. John Chrysostom, *Homilies on Romans*, trans. Panayiotis Papageorgiou, vol. 1 (Brookline, MA: Holy Cross Orthodox, 2013), 10.17–20.

5. "The Nicene Creed," in *Creeds, Confessions, and Catechisms: A Reader's Edition*, ed. Chad Van Dixhoorn (Wheaton, IL: Crossway, 2022), 17.

Stott says, "The essence of sin is man substituting himself for God, while the essence of salvation is God substituting himself for man."[6] At the heart of Christianity is the triune God's work of "at-one-ment" through substitution. As the new Adam and the true Israel, Jesus died in our place.[7]

At one level, this is the simple message of the gospel: "Christ died for our sins" (1 Cor. 15:3). But we must press deeper. The gospel is a fresh drink of water to parched souls, but it is also an ocean of meaning within which one can swim. Why did Jesus die in our place? How does his death achieve our salvation? Where is this in Scripture? Does the history of the church attest to substitutionary atonement? Answering these questions will bring us to the very heart of the doctrine of atonement.

Substitution in the Old Testament

The substitutionary work of Christ is incomprehensible apart from the Old Testament. Jesus himself said, "The Son of Man goes as it is written of him" (Mark 14:21), revealing that his life was fulfilling the divine script of the Old Testament. And at the heart of this story is Israel's hope for a Messiah.

The Messiah was the Spirit-anointed King of Israel who would reclaim God's reign over all of creation. As the son of God (2 Sam. 7:12–14) and son of man (Dan. 7:1–14), the Messiah was the promised one who would set right all that our sin made wrong, reconciling sinners to God, defeating evil, and renewing heaven and earth. While much could be said about the Messiah and his mission, we will highlight the Old Testament's witness to the Messiah being our substitute, the one who

---

6. John Stott, *The Cross of Christ* (Downers Grove, IL: InterVarsity Press, 1986), 160.

7. Jesus can only be our substitute because he is first our representative as the new Adam and the true Israel. Therefore, substitution and representation go hand in hand. Christ died in our place *instead of us* (substitution) and *with us* (representation). Christ's representative work in atonement will be discussed in chapter 6.

would suffer in our place for our sins. Substitution in the Old Testament can be seen in three ways: a narrative pattern, the sacrificial system, and messianic prophecies.

There is a *narrative pattern* throughout the Old Testament where God's kingdom promises are fulfilled through substitution and sacrifice. The seed of the woman will crush the serpent while being bruised in the process (Gen. 3:15). The beloved son of Abraham is spared because the ram dies in his place (Gen. 22:13). In the exodus, the unblemished lamb dies in place of all the firstborn to redeem Israel (Ex. 12). Moses offers his own life to the Lord as a substitutionary sacrifice on behalf of Israel (Ex. 32:30–32). The servant in Isaiah gives his life as a sacrificial offering to make the many righteous (Isa. 53:8–12). This narrative pattern points forward to Christ, our once-for-all substitute. Jesus is the beloved Son, the unblemished Lamb, the prophet who stands in the gap, and the sacrifice that atones for our sins.

This narrative pattern of substitution and sacrifice was institutionalized in Israel's *sacrificial system*. Through sacrifices and offerings, unholy people could once again dwell with a holy God. The centrality of atonement in the sacrificial system is evident in the frequent use of the Hebrew verb *kipper* throughout Leviticus, which is usually translated, "to make atonement." According to Jay Sklar, *kipper* refers to "ransom-purification"— that which rescues sinful humanity from the wrath of God (ransom) and cleanses their sin (purification).[8] While not all offerings and sacrifices in the Old Testament are substitutionary, most involve shedding blood and bearing the consequences of sin on behalf of sinners.[9] Of particular significance was the Day

---

8. Jay Sklar, *Leviticus: An Introduction and Commentary*, Tyndale Old Testament Commentaries (Downers Grove, IL: IVP Academic, 2014), 53.

9. In the Old Testament, there are many different types of offerings (burnt, grain, peace, sin, guilt) and sacrifices (burnt, peace, sin, guilt).

of Atonement (Lev. 16). Once a year, on the Day of Atonement, two goats would be offered on behalf of the people. The first goat would be sacrificed and its blood sprinkled to atone for the Holy Place, the altar, and the tent of meeting. The priest would place his hands on the head of the second goat, confessing all the sins of the people, and the goat would then be sent into the wilderness to "bear all their iniquities on itself" (Lev. 16:22). Together, these sacrifices would make atonement (*kipper*) for the sins of the people, paying the debt of their sin (ransom) and cleansing them before the Lord (purification) (Lev. 16:30). The New Testament makes clear that the entire sacrificial system could not fully atone for sins and was pointing forward to Jesus who would be the once-for-all sacrifice of atonement (Heb. 10:1). Christ is the sacrifice who dies in our place to pay our debt and cleanse our sin. He bears our iniquities and enters exile so that we might be brought home with the Lord. The sacrificial nature of Christ's death is so significant in the New Testament that the "blood of Christ" is mentioned three times as often as his "cross" and five times as often as his "death." As the author of Hebrews says, "Without the shedding of blood there is no forgiveness of sin" (Heb. 9:22).[10]

Substitution is also seen in *messianic prophecies* throughout the Old Testament (e.g., Dan. 9:24–27; Zech. 9:9–11; 12:10; 13:1). Among the passages that reveal the substitutionary nature of the Messiah's work, however, Isaiah 53 is of utmost importance. As we have seen, the context of Isaiah 53 reveals that God's kingdom will come about through the counterintui-

---

10. Leviticus 17:11 is crucial for understanding the role of blood in atonement: "For the life of the flesh is in the blood, and I have given it for you on the altar to make atonement for your souls, for it is the blood that makes atonement by the life." The interpretive question for this verse is whether "blood" is referring to life or death. Some scholars argue that blood refers to life and, therefore, that Christ's life (not death) is salvific. Others argue that blood is referring to death. I believe it is both. The blood represents life given. The blood of a sacrifice is not blood within a living body but rather blood that is shed as a part of sacrificial death.

tive means of a suffering servant. And while there are many complexities to this rich passage, the substitutionary nature of the servant is inescapable.

> *He* was pierced for *our* transgressions;
>> *he* was crushed for *our* iniquities;
> upon *him* was the chastisement that brought *us* peace,
>> and with *his* wounds *we* are healed. (Isa. 53:5)

What a wonderful exchange. And while Isaiah 53:5 is the apex of the theme, substitution is embedded throughout the song:

- "*He* has borne *our* griefs" (Isa. 53:4).
- "The LORD has laid on *him* the iniquity of *us* all" (Isa. 53:6).
- "*He* shall bear *their* iniquities" (Isa. 53:11).
- "*He* . . . was numbered with the *transgressors*" (Isa. 53:12).
- "*He* bore the sin of *many*" (Isa. 53:12).

By suffering in their place, the servant will atone for the sins of God's people, bringing about a new exodus and establishing God's kingdom.[11]

Substitution in the New Testament

The resurrected Jesus explained the meaning of his death by leading his disciples through the Old Testament, demonstrating that the Christ must suffer and rise from the dead (Luke

---

11. Although the noun "atonement" (*kippur*) is not in Isaiah 53, the concept is clearly present, as seen in the language of making an offering for guilt (Isa. 53:10) and bearing iniquities/sins (Isa. 53:11–12). Alan Groves says, "The language of Isaiah 53 is indeed atonement language since it concerns that which purifies and shields from Yahweh's wrath." J. Alan Groves, "Atonement in Isaiah 53: For He Bore the Sins of Many," in *The Glory of the Atonement: Biblical, Historical and Practical Perspectives; Essays in Honor of Roger Nicole*, ed. Charles E. Hill and Frank A. James III (Downers Grove, IL: IVP Academic, 2004), 68.

24:26–27, 44–46). While Christ was referring to the pattern throughout the Old Testament, two passages in particular reveal how he understood his death as substitutionary.

Christ's definitive statement on the meaning of his death—"the Son of Man came not to be served but to serve, and to give his life as a ransom for many" (Mark 10:45)—alludes to Isaiah 53 with references to Jesus's identity as the "servant" (Isa. 52:13) and his suffering for "the many" (Isa. 53:12). The New Testament authors carried on what they learned from their master. Matthew and John refer to Isaiah 53 to understand Jesus's ministry (Matt. 8:17; John 12:38). Acts 8 demonstrates that the early church interpreted Christ's death in light of Isaiah 53. When an Ethiopian eunuch was perplexed by reading Isaiah 53, a disciple of Jesus approached him and "beginning with this Scripture [Isa. 53:7–8] he told him the good news about Jesus" (Acts 8:35). Paul echoes many of the themes from Isaiah 53 when he speaks of Christ's work, and he explicitly references the suffering servant in Romans 10:16. Peter interprets Christ's death by directly referring to several parts of the song of the suffering servant, declaring, "By his wounds you have been healed" (1 Pet. 2:24). The substitutionary nature of the servant's suffering is deeply embedded into the New Testament's understanding of atonement.

Jesus also explained the meaning of his death by referring to the unblemished lamb in the exodus story (Ex. 12). The night before he was crucified, Jesus shared the Passover meal with his disciples. But when he broke the bread, he said, "This is my body" (Matt. 26:26). He then took the cup, saying, "This is my blood of the covenant, which is poured out for many for the forgiveness of sins" (Matt. 26:28). Jesus was reconfiguring the Passover story around himself, showing that he was bringing about a new exodus and establishing an eternal kingdom. As N. T. Wright says, "When Jesus wanted to explain to his followers what his forthcoming death was all about, he did not give them a theory, a model, a metaphor, or any other such thing; he gave them a meal."[12] The apostle Paul also interprets Christ's death in light of the exodus, declaring that "Christ, our Passover lamb, has been sacrificed" (1 Cor. 5:7). Jesus is the spotless Lamb whose blood covers God's people and spares them from God's judgment.

The New Testament authors sum up the meaning of Christ's suffering by declaring that he died "for" us. Christ . . .

- "died *for* the ungodly" (Rom. 5:6);
- "gave himself *for* me" (Gal. 2:20);
- "suffered *for* you" (1 Pet. 2:21);
- "lays down his life *for* the sheep" (John 10:11);
- "gave himself up *for* us" (Eph. 5:2);
- "laid down his life *for* us" (1 John 3:16);
- "gave himself *for* us" (Titus 2:14);
- "died *for* us" (Rom. 5:8; 1 Thess. 5:10).

The preposition "for" in all these verses is the Greek *hyper*, which generally means "on behalf of" but can also mean "in the place of" or "instead of."[13] One example where *hyper* certainly refers to substitution is 1 Peter 3:18: "Christ also suffered once for sins, the righteous for [*hyper*] the unrighteous, that he might bring us to God." Furthermore, while *hyper* is the most common preposition used when discussing Christ's death "for" us, according to Mark, Jesus used the word *anti*, which means

---

12. N. T. Wright, *The Day the Revolution Began: Reconsidering the Meaning of Jesus's Crucifixion* (San Francisco: HarperOne, 2016), 182.

13. Walter Bauer, *A Greek-English Lexicon of the New Testament and Other Early Christian Literature*, rev. and ed. Frederick William Gingrich, 3rd ed. (Chicago: University of Chicago Press, 2000), s.v. "ὑπέρ."

"instead of" or "in place of," to describe the meaning of his death as a "ransom *for* many" (Mark 10:45).[14]

Of course, the idea of substitution is not bound by a word. The concept is prevalent throughout the New Testament and explicit in at least the following verses:

> For our sake he made him to be sin who knew no sin, so that in him we might become the righteousness of God. (2 Cor. 5:21)

> Christ redeemed us from the curse of the law by becoming a curse for us—for it is written, "Cursed is everyone who is hanged on a tree." (Gal. 3:13)[15]

Substitution in Church History

Substitutionary atonement is not a modern development but rather has been affirmed throughout church history. The following is a sampling of representative figures from different eras.

The Epistle to Diognetus, written in the second century, declares, "O the sweet exchange, O the incomprehensible work of God, O the unexpected blessings, that the sinfulness of many should be hidden in one righteous person, while the righteousness of one should justify many sinners!" (Diogn. 9:5).[16]

Athanasius argues that Christ offered himself as "a sufficient exchange for all." He says,

---

14. The declaration that Christ died "for us" is also nuanced in Scripture by the affirmation that Christ died "for *our sins*" (1 Cor. 15:3; Gal. 1:4), meaning that Christ died because of our sins and to deal with our sins.

15. For a review of criticisms regarding substitution and a defense of substitution in Scripture, see Simon Gathercole, *Defending Substitution: An Essay on Atonement in Paul* (Grand Rapids, MI: Baker Academic, 2015).

16. "The Epistle to Diognetus," in *The Apostolic Fathers: Greek Texts and English Translations*, ed. and trans. Michael W. Holmes, 3rd ed. (Grand Rapids, MI: Baker Academic, 2007), 711.

It was by surrendering to death the body which He had taken, as an offering and sacrifice free from every stain, that He forthwith abolished death for His human brethren by the offering of the equivalent. For naturally, since the Word of God was above all, when He offered His own temple and bodily instrument as a substitute for the life of all, He fulfilled in death all that was required.[17]

Augustine says, "Christ, though guiltless, took our punishment, that he might cancel our guilt, and do away with our punishment."[18] According to Thomas Aquinas, "Now it is a fitting way of satisfying for another to submit oneself to the penalty deserved by that other. And so Christ resolved to die, that by dying He might atone for us."[19] Martin Luther says, "This is that mystery which is rich in divine grace unto sinners; wherein, by a wonderful exchange, our sins are now no longer ours but Christ's: and the righteousness of Christ is ours."[20] John and Charles Wesley championed Christ's substitutionary work in their sermons, writings, and hymns. Charles Wesley's hymn "Wherewith, O Lord, Shall I Draw Near?" is a representative example:

Jesus, the Lamb of God, hath bled,
He bore our sins upon the tree,
Beneath our curse He bowed His head,
'Tis finished! He hath died for me![21]

---

17. Athanasius, *On the Incarnation*, trans. and ed. a Religious of C.S.M.V. (Crestwood, NY: St. Vladimir's Seminary Press, 2002), 35 (2.9).

18. Augustine, *Against Faustus*, in vol. 4 of *Nicene and Post-Nicene Fathers*, Series 1, ed. Philip Schaff (Grand Rapids, MI: Eerdmans, 1974), 207 (14.1).

19. Thomas Aquinas, *Summa Theologica*, trans. Fathers of the English Dominican Province (New York: Benziger Bros, 1947), 3.50.1.

20. Martin Luther, *Select Works of Martin Luther: An Offering to the Church of God in "the Last Days"*, trans. Henry Cole (London: W. Simpkin and R. Marshall, 1826), 4:369.

21. Charles Wesley, "Wherewith, O Lord, Shall I Draw Near?," 1866.

The Swiss theologian Karl Barth offers a thoroughly substitutionary approach to Christ's work. According to Barth, the Son of God is "the judge judged in our place."[22] He also writes, "Man's reconciliation with God takes place through God putting Himself in man's place and man's being put in God's place, as a sheer act of grace."[23]

A contemporary Nigerian scholar, Yusufu Turaki, offers an example of how this understanding of substitutionary atonement is not only common throughout generations but also across cultures: "By taking humanity's sins in his body on the cross and by dying for our sake, Jesus Christ became our substitute and paid in full the wages of our sins."[24]

How Does Substitution Deal with Sin?

While Scripture clearly teaches *that* Christ is our substitute, we must still ask *how* his substitutionary death achieves our salvation. To find an answer, let us remember that the human dilemma is multidimensional (sin leaves humanity in bondage to the evil one, blind to the truth, hostile toward one another, and so on) with the core problem being that sin has ruptured the divine/human relationship.

The core problem—our fractured communion with God—has two sides. From humanity's side, it is marked by rebellion and idolatry. We have rejected God and looked to the creation rather than the Creator for our joy and satisfaction. The other side of the problem is that God's holy, loving, fitting-with-his-character response to sin is judgment. Just as a good judge would not let the guilty go free, God holds humanity account-

---

22. Karl Barth, *The Doctrine of Reconciliation*, vol. 4/1 of *Church Dogmatics*, ed. G. W. Bromiley and Thomas Torrance, trans. G. W. Bromiley (Edinburgh: T&T Clark, 1958), 211.
23. Karl Barth, *Dogmatics in Outline* (New York: Harper Torchbooks, 1959), 115.
24. Yusufu Turaki, *Engaging Religions and Worldviews in Africa: A Christian Theological Method* (Bukuru, Nigeria: HippoBooks, 2020), 315.

able for sin. The Lord is "merciful and gracious, slow to anger, and abounding in steadfast love and faithfulness . . . but [he] will by no means clear the guilty" (Ex. 34:6–7).

God is a good King who loves his creation and is, therefore, opposed to that which violates its goodness. Because of his love (not in spite of it), God responds to sin and wickedness with anger. God's wrath is not a divine temper tantrum but is rather his holy, settled opposition to that which seeks to corrode his creation. God's response to sin, therefore, is judgment (2 Cor. 5:10), punishment (2 Thess. 1:9), wrath (John 3:36), a curse (Deut. 11:28), exile (2 Kings 17:6–7), and ultimately death (Rom. 6:23). This is the penalty of sin.

Here is where the logic of substitution reveals the *how* of atonement. By dying in our place, Jesus takes on himself what we deserve: judgment (Rom. 8:3), punishment (Isa. 53:5), wrath (1 Thess. 1:10), a curse (Gal. 3:13), exile (Heb. 13:12), and ultimately death (Heb. 2:14). He pays the penalty for our sin, and we receive the immeasurable riches of his grace. We share in his sonship (Eph. 1:5), receive his righteousness (2 Cor. 5:21), and are filled with his Spirit (Rom. 8:9).[25]

By dealing with our sin against God, Christ's substitution is the key that then unlocks the many dimensions of the atonement: disarming the powers (Col. 2:13–15), demonstrating God's love (Rom. 5:8), providing an example (1 Pet. 2:21)— in fact, all of creation will experience redemption on the coattails of what God has done to reconcile humanity to himself (Rom. 8:18–25).

---

25. Some may wonder why I do not include *penal* in front of substitution when I talk about the heart of atonement. First, while I gladly affirm penal substitution with appropriate nuances and qualifications, I am not primarily working at the level of theories, and penal substitution is a theory (actually, there are many different theories of penal substitution). Second, the penal aspect is indispensable to but not exhaustive of the meaning of substitution. Substitution is penal, but it is also propitiatory, victorious, and so on. In other words, substitution is the heart of atonement, and substitution is certainly penal. But that is different than saying the theory of penal substitution is the heart of atonement.

The Self-Giving Love of the Triune God

Substitution has often unfortunately been portrayed in crude and unhelpful ways. Take, for example, the common sermon illustration of the train conductor whose son is innocently playing in the gears that shift the railroad tracks. As the train approaches and the conductor realizes his son is in the gears, he has a dilemma. Either the father spares his son and allows the train to go off the tracks, surely leading to the demise of all those on the train. Or he shifts the gears, sacrificing his own son to save those on the train. The conductor, as the story is told, sacrifices his son to save those on the train. He died so that they could live.

While this illustration does communicate the idea of sacrifice, it smuggles in with it other assumptions that are detrimental to a biblical understanding of atonement. In the story, the son does not willingly die but is rather blindsided by his father. The father in this story is not driven by love (he apparently knows nothing of those in the train) but rather by a utilitarian principle of doing what is best for the greatest number of people.

Many other illustrations or approaches unintentionally portray the atonement as an exchange between an angry Father and a loving Son. In order for sin to be dealt with, either the Son has to persuade the Father, or the Father has to obliterate the Son. Again, while there are elements of truth in these approaches (the Father does get angry, and the Son is loving), they are deeply flawed because they pit Father against Son in a way that undermines the very nature of God as revealed in Scripture.

We must remember that the cross is the apex of the atoning mission of the triune God. To rightly understand the atonement, we need to see substitution as the self-giving love of Father, Son, and Holy Spirit. As Paul says, *God in Christ* was reconciling the world to himself (2 Cor. 5:19). In giving his Son, God gave himself. The Father and Son are of one accord in their atoning mission—the Father motivated by love (John 3:16) and the Son voluntarily giving his life in complete harmony with the purposes of the Father (John 10:18). And the Holy Spirit is at work throughout Christ's atoning mission. Jesus was led and empowered by the Spirit throughout his perfect life and ministry (Luke 4:1). He offered his blood "through the eternal Spirit" (Heb. 9:14), and he was resurrected from the dead by the power of the Spirit (Rom. 8:11). John Stott is right in saying that the cross is the "self-substitution of God."[26]

While the doctrine of atonement is centered on Christ, we cannot think of Jesus as an independent individual but as the Son of the Father who is empowered by the Spirit. Atonement is a work of the triune God through and through. On the cross, Father, Son, and Holy Spirit were at work together for the salvation of sinners.[27] Two classic Trinitarian principles must guide our thinking here. First, the principle of inseparable operations teaches that all external works of the Trinity

---

26. Stott, *The Cross of Christ*, 133.

27. One may ask, did God punish Jesus? The answer to this question requires much nuance and an awareness of the way in which such a claim can be misunderstood. Furthermore, Rom. 8:3 says that God "condemned *sin* in the flesh" of Jesus. In other words, the emphasis is on God's punishment of sin in the flesh of Christ, not the Father punishing the Son. The Father does not hate the Son but rather loves the Son, even as the Son bears the punishment deserved by sinners. As I have tried to emphasize, we must understand the cross within a Trinitarian framework. Therefore, I think it would be more wise to say that God in Christ bore our punishment because of his love. Herman Bavinck says, "It is completely true that Christ was never personally—on account of his own self—the object of God's wrath. The reason, of course, is that he was never in his own person a sinner, a violator of God's law." Herman Bavinck, *Sin and Salvation in Christ*, vol. 3 of *Reformed Dogmatics*, ed. John Bolt, trans. John Vriend (Grand Rapids, MI: Baker Academic, 2003), 399. According to John Calvin, "Yet we do not suggest that God was ever inimical or angry toward him. How could he be angry toward his beloved Son, 'in whom his heart reposed' [cf. Matt. 3:17]? How could Christ by his intercession appease the Father toward others, if he were himself hateful to God? This is what we are saying: he bore the weight of divine severity, since he was 'stricken and afflicted' (cf. Isa. 53:5) by God's hand, and experienced all the signs of a wrathful and avenging God." John Calvin, *Institutes of the Christian Religion*, ed. John T. McNeill, trans. Ford Lewis Battles, 2 vols., Library of Christian Classics (Louisville: Westminster John Knox, 2006), 1:517 (2.16.11).

are undivided. This is not merely an aspect of what God does but rather the essence of who he is. God *is* triune. Second, the principle of appropriation enables us to designate certain works primarily to the Father or the Son or the Spirit. So while creation is an act of the triune God, we can say more specifically that the Father creates through the Son by the Spirit. The principle of inseparable operations emphasizes that on the cross it was *God* in Christ reconciling the world to himself. The principle of appropriation emphasizes that it was God *in Christ* at work on the cross.[28]

Taking all this into account, by "substitution" we mean the self-giving of the triune God in Christ. Stott sums it up well: "In and through Christ crucified God substituted himself for us and bore our sins, dying in our place the death we deserved to die, in order that we might be restored to his favour and adopted into his family."[29] God's triune nature is essential for understanding substitutionary atonement. Otherwise, one may end up pitting Father against Son, as if either the Son had to pacify an angry deity or the Father had to sacrifice an unwilling Son. God in Christ has given himself in order to atone for sins, reconcile sinners to himself, and renew all of creation.

---

28. One may wonder how this applies to Christ's cry of dereliction on the cross, "My God, my God, why have you forsaken me?" (Mark 15:34). This has often been preached, rather crudely, as a "break in the Trinity," as if God divided into two parts over the weekend, somehow ceasing to be God, and then mystically reunited to resume his divine agenda. Two factors must be kept in mind as one reads the cry of dereliction. First, God's triune mission provides the proper theological context for Christ's words. And the doctrine of the Trinity describes not an attribute of God but the essence of God. As I have emphasized, the atonement is a united work of Father, Son, and Holy Spirit from beginning to end. Second, Christ's cry is a quote of Ps. 22:1 and refers to the psalm in its entirety. Psalm 22 is a cry of lament from a righteous sufferer that expresses pain and forsakenness within a broader framework of trust and redemption. In fact, in Ps. 22:24 the psalmist says, "For he has not despised or abhorred / the affliction of the afflicted, / and he has not hidden his face from him, / but has heard, when he cried to him." Christ's cry of dereliction truly does represent Jesus entering into exile and forsakenness on behalf of humanity, but within a broader Trinitarian work of God bearing the punishment of his people in Christ. See Thomas McCall, *Forsaken: The Trinity and the Cross, and Why It Matters* (Downers Grove, IL: IVP Academic, 2012).

29. Stott, *The Cross of Christ*, 7.

Not Only Our Substitute in Death

Thus far in this chapter, we have focused on the way in which substitution is the *how* of the atonement. Christ died in our place for our sins. However, Christ's death by itself could not have dealt with the problem of sin, and substitution is not limited to the cross of Christ. As John Webster says, "No one moment of the history can bear the weight of the whole."[30] We must see how Christ is our substitute in all of his work. And we also must be able to connect each aspect of his ministry to the cross as an integrated work. In the remainder of this chapter we will explore how Christ's substitutionary work encompasses the spectrum of his ministry.

The Cradle and the Cross

The Son of God could not have dealt with our sins from heaven. He had to come to earth. Christ could not be our mediator without becoming like us in every way. He had to take on flesh. Without the incarnation, the atonement is impossible. As Hebrews 2:17 says, "He had to be made like his brothers in every respect, so that he might become a merciful and faithful high priest in the service of God, to make propitiation for the sins of the people."

Regarding the incarnation, Gregory Nazianzus writes, "The unassumed is the unhealed."[31] In other words, if Jesus did not have a human mind, he could not heal our minds. If he did not take on a human body, he could not heal our bodies. If he

---

30. John Webster, "Rector et Index Super Omnia Genera Doctrinarum? The Place of the Doctrine of Justification," in *What Is Justification About? Reformed Contributions to an Ecumenical Theme*, ed. Michael Weinrich and John Burgess (Grand Rapids, MI: Eerdmans, 2009), 41.

31. Gregory of Nazianzus, "Letter 101: The First Letter to Cledonius the Presbyter," in *On God and Christ: The Five Theological Orations and Two Letters to Cledonius*, trans. Frederick Williams and Lionel Wickham (Crestwood: St. Vladimir's Seminary Press, 2002), 158.

did not have a human soul, then he could not heal our soul. Jesus had to be fully God and fully human to be the mediator between God and humanity. "For there is one God, and there is one mediator between God and men, the man Christ Jesus, who gave himself as a ransom for all" (1 Tim. 2:5–6).

It is not enough to say that the incarnation is merely a necessary prelude to the atonement. The incarnation is itself part of the atonement. As John Calvin says,

> How has Christ abolished sin? . . . He has achieved this for us by the whole course of his obedience. . . . In short, from the time when he took on the form of a servant, he began to pay the price of liberation in order to redeem us.
>
> Yet to define salvation more exactly, Scripture ascribes this as peculiar and proper to Christ's death.[32]

Calvin affirms Christ's taking on flesh as a part of his atoning work. Yet he also locates it within a broader narrative where the cross is central to the atonement. The cradle ultimately points to the cross. As Athanasius argues, Jesus is the eternal Son of God who is incapable of death. Therefore, the author of life took on a body so that he might offer it up as a sacrifice to deal with the sin of humanity.[33] The cross is the apex of the incarnate Christ's mission.

A Cross-Shaped Life

The life of Christ is often overlooked in atonement studies. But if Jesus does not live a covenant-keeping, sinless life, then there is no atonement. Christ is our substitute not only in bearing the penalty for our breaking the law through his death but also in keeping the law on our behalf through his perfect life.

---

32. Calvin, *Institutes*, 1:507 (2.16.5).
33. Athanasius, *On the Incarnation*, 35 (2.9).

To say that Jesus was perfect means that he always kept God's covenant, never broke God's law, and lived for the glory of God with every thought, attitude, and action. Jesus was "without sin" (Heb. 4:15), and in all that he did he loved God and neighbor. Yet his perfect life is *for us*. He kept the covenant on our behalf so that, by grace, his perfect life could be reckoned to us (2 Cor. 5:21). His life is a substitute for ours. We are given his righteousness, covenant-keeping record, and status as beloved children of God.

Through his perfect life, Jesus was recapitulating the stories of Adam and Israel, being faithful at every step of the journey where they were unfaithful. While Adam chose his own way in the garden of Eden, Jesus chose God's way in the garden of Gethsemane. While Israel was overcome by temptation in the wilderness, Jesus resisted temptation in the wilderness. While Adam and Israel abandoned the mission of the kingdom, Jesus embodied the kingdom. Jesus is the new Adam and true Israel, perfectly fulfilling in his life the calling of humanity.

The ministry of Christ was filled with miracles, healings, exorcisms, and teachings. But all these signs of the kingdom were pointing forward to the in-breaking of the kingdom through the cross. Jesus cast out many demons throughout his life, but the exorcism of Satan came through Christ's death (John 12:31). Jesus healed many people throughout his ministry, but it is ultimately through his wounds that we are healed (Isa. 53:5). Jesus gave sight to the blind, but it was only as he was crucified that someone truly saw his identity as the Son of God (Mark 15:39).

The life and death of Jesus are intricately related in the Scriptures. Through his death, Christ was offering his life. Yet, throughout his life, the suffering of his death was already underway. In fact, Jesus was born into a world that was trying to take his life. Whether it was Herod's attempt at infanticide

(Matt. 2:16), a crowd's effort to throw Jesus off a cliff (Luke 4:29), or the Pharisees' desire to destroy him (Matt. 12:14), the suffering of the cross casts a shadow all the way back to the manger. In this sense, we can say that Christ's whole life has a cruciform shape to it. As Bavinck says, "Christ's entire life and work, from his conception to his death, was substitutionary in nature."[34] Through his covenant-keeping life and curse-bearing death, Jesus atones for sin and makes sinners right with God.

The Resurrection of the Crucified

Jesus's death on the cross changed the world in a moment and its trajectory for eternity. The kingdom had come. The mission had been fulfilled. Human history was altered forever.

But hardly anyone noticed.

The onlookers of the crucifixion naturally assumed that death was loss, darkness was defeat, and the kingdom mission had come to a bloody halt.

Until Jesus rose from the grave.

The resurrection of the crucified Savior was evidence that Christ's weakness was power, his sacrifice was victory, and he was, in fact, a King enthroned on an old rugged cross. People often think of the resurrection as a last-minute triumph that unexpectedly saved the day after Christ was conquered on the cross. But this misconstrues Christ's work. The cross is not a defeat that is made right by the resurrection but a victory that is revealed in the resurrection. The identity and mission of Christ were vindicated when he walked out of the tomb.[35]

---

34. Bavinck, *Sin and Salvation in Christ*, 378.

35. People often refer to Rom. 4:25 to argue that the resurrection is the basis of justification: Jesus was "raised for our justification." However, a deeper study of the Greek text of the verse offers a different and more likely interpretation. N. T. Wright explains, "It isn't that the resurrection of Jesus causes that 'justification.' Rather, it is the sign that this justification has in principle taken place on the cross." Wright, *The Day the Revolution Began*, 323.

The resurrection is also the beginning of the new creation. The work of the cross was finished, but its accomplishment still needed to be inaugurated and implemented, which is exactly what happened through the resurrection. On the first Easter Sunday, the doors of the cruciform kingdom were flung wide open to a world decaying in sin. As the Indian theologian Idicheria Ninan says, "The resurrection involved far more than just the resuscitation of a corpse! It marks the inauguration of a new era in the history of God's saving interventions, the climax of God's covenant with Abraham and the beginning of a new creation."[36] The resurrection of Christ is the beginning of the renovation of the cosmos.

Jesus is—and always will be—the risen King. But he also continues to be the crucified King. In fact, when Jesus's disciples encountered the resurrected Christ, it was the signs of his death that revealed his identity to them. Thomas did not believe until he placed his hands in Jesus's scars (John 20:26–29). The two disciples on the road to Emmaus did not recognize the risen Christ until they saw in the Scriptures that "the Christ should suffer these things and enter into his glory" (Luke 24:26). The book of Revelation reveals Christ as our glorious King, but he is still the slain Lamb on the throne. Jesus is forever our crucified and risen King.

Comprehending the relationship between Christ's crucifixion and resurrection is essential for the doctrine of atonement. The cross and empty tomb are not in competition with one another but represent different aspects of a unified work. Jesus's death is "for our sins" (1 Cor. 15:3), and his resurrection is the beginning of the new creation (1 Cor. 15:20). Together, they are "of first importance" (1 Cor. 15:3).

---

36. Idicheria Ninan, "Ephesians," in *South Asia Bible Commentary*, ed. Brian Wintle (Grand Rapids, MI: Zondervan, 2015), 1636.

The Ascension of the Crucified and Resurrected Christ

The crucified and risen Christ ascended to the right hand of the Father and is now reigning over all creation. Christ's return to heaven, however, represents several aspects of his heavenly ministry: ascension, heavenly offering, session, Pentecost, and intercession.

The ascension is significant for the atonement because it plays a key role in the union of heaven and earth. While the world was made to have heaven and earth overlapping and God dwelling with his people, sin brought about a great rift. But when Christ ascended into the heavenly realm, those in Christ ascended with him. Followers of Jesus, therefore, are simultaneously on earth and seated with Christ in the heavenly realm (Eph. 2:6). Christ, as the new Adam, has ascended to heaven, thereby leading humanity upward toward our original purpose of union with God.[37] In this sense, just as Christ died and rose *for us*, he also ascended *for us*. The "at-one-ment" of heaven and earth comes about through the divine Son descending to bring heaven to humanity and then ascending to bring humanity into heaven.

When Christ ascended, a key aspect of his atoning work was the offering of his blood in the heavenly sanctuary (Heb. 9:11–14). Some scholars believe this refers to a heavenly perspective coinciding with Christ's shedding of blood on the cross, while others argue that it is something that happens later in time in heaven.[38] Either way, the heavenly offering of the blood

---

37. See Douglas Farrow, *Ascension Theology* (New York: T&T Clark, 2011), 1–14.

38. For example, Thomas R. Schreiner argues that Christ's self-offering takes place at the cross and the heavenly offering in Heb. 9:23–25 is symbolically referring to the effectiveness of Christ's death. Thomas R. Schreiner, *Commentary on Hebrews*, Biblical Theology for Christian Proclamation (Nashville: Holman, 2015), 283–85. David Moffitt, on the other hand, argues that according to Hebrews, atonement is not accomplished on the cross but in the heavenly sanctuary, where the resurrected Jesus presents his life (not death) on the altar. David Moffitt, *Atonement and the Logic of Resurrection in the Epistle to the Hebrews*, Supplements to Novum Testamentum 141 (Leiden: Brill, 2011), 294.

of Christ is significant for the atonement. As the Old Testament sacrificial system makes clear, atonement is a process that includes not only the shedding of blood but also the offering of blood (either poured out or sprinkled). Therefore, the shedding of blood on the cross and the offering of blood in the heavenly tabernacle ought not be pit against one another but seen as crucial parts of the same process that results in atonement.

Psalm 110 tells of the Messiah being seated at the right hand of God in heaven. This messianic priest-king will share in God's reign and rule over God's enemies. The significance of the session of the Messiah is evident from the fact that Psalm 110:1 is the most frequently quoted Old Testament passage in the entire New Testament. The session of Christ symbolizes not only that he accomplished his mission (he sat down) but also that he continues to reign (he sat down *on a throne*). As the book of Revelation portrays Christ, he is the slain Lamb on the throne.

How does Christ reign from heaven? He reigns through the Spirit. Jesus poured out the Holy Spirit on his disciples in order to apply his finished work, bringing about the renewal that will one day reach the ends of the earth. As Thomas F. Torrance says, "*Pentecost belongs to the atonement*, for the presence of the Spirit is the actualisation amongst us of the new or redeemed life."[39] Without Pentecost, atonement means nothing.

We have been discussing what Christ has already done. He ascended. He offered his blood. He sat down. He sent the Spirit. But what is Jesus doing now? He is praying for his people. Romans 8:34 says, "Who is to condemn? Christ Jesus is the one

---

I am inclined to follow R. B. Jamieson, who argues that Christ's self-offering takes place in the heavenly sanctuary but that he is offering the accomplishment of his atoning death on the cross. R. B. Jamieson, *Jesus' Death and Heavenly Offering in Hebrews*, Society for New Testament Studies Monograph Series 172 (Cambridge: Cambridge University Press, 2019).

39. Thomas F. Torrance, *Atonement: The Person and Work of Christ*, ed. Robert Walker (Downers Grove, IL: IVP Academic, 2009), 178 (emphasis in original).

who died—more than that, who was raised—who is at the right hand of God, who indeed is interceding for us." Jesus is not dispassionately waiting in heaven until we arrive. He is interceding for his weary followers who have experienced his grace but still bend under the pressures of a fallen world. What does this have to do with atonement? While it is through Christ's atoning death that we are adopted into the family of God, it is through his ongoing intercession that we are able to continually draw near to the one whom we now call "Father." Jesus is our forever high priest who has saved us to the uttermost and "always lives to make intercession" for his people (Heb. 7:25).

The Return of the Lamb

While the atoning work of Christ was finished on the cross, it will not be consummated until Christ returns to judge the living and the dead. The second coming of Christ, therefore, is not merely a step beyond the atonement but rather is its closing piece. This is why the book of Revelation constantly refers to the reigning and returning Christ as the Lamb. Jesus is the slain Lamb on the throne who will return to renew all things and celebrate the marriage supper of the Lamb with his redeemed people from every tribe and tongue. The reconciliation of sinners and God, along with the "at-one-ment" of heaven and earth, will be fully realized when Christ returns to make all things new.

In sum, the atonement achieved by Christ encompasses his work from conception to consummation and centers on his death on the cross.

3

The Achievements
of Atonement

A Multidimensional Work

Bless the LORD, *O my soul,*
 and forget not all his benefits,
who forgives all your iniquity,
 who heals all your diseases,
who redeems your life from the pit,
 who crowns you with steadfast love and mercy,
who satisfies you with good
 so that your youth is renewed like the eagle's.
PSALM 103:2–5

Jesus inaugurated the kingdom on the cross, which
would enable us to understand better the gospel's integral
content and the atonement's kaleidoscopic images.[1]
PRABO MIHINDUKULASURIYA

---

1. Prabo Mihindukulasuriya, "How Jesus Inaugurated the Kingdom on the Cross: A Kingdom Perspective of the Atonement," *Evangelical Review of Theology* 38, no. 3 (2014): 197.

The death of Christ is a multidimensional accomplishment within the story of God's kingdom coming on earth as it is in heaven. Having explored substitution as the *how* of atonement, we can now turn our attention to *what* Christ accomplished. Substitution is the heart but not the whole of the atonement. Christ dying in our place and for our sins results in a multiplicity of achievements.

The Problem of One-Dimensional Reductionism

The trend in modern atonement theology has been to compress Christ's atoning work into singular, exclusive theories, as if Christ *either* bore our punishment (penal substitution) *or* conquered evil (*Christus Victor*) *or* demonstrated his love as an example (moral exemplarism). The problem with this approach is that it truncates the gospel and forces people to choose between half-truths as opposed to embracing the whole truth. Unfortunately, pendulum-swinging debates have furthered the divide between one-dimensional theories and reduced the fullness of the truth to a fraction of reality.

A Multidimensional Approach

The church needs an approach to the doctrine of atonement where the various dimensions of Christ's work are all appreciated and seen as complementary rather than competitive, seeking to do justice to the fullness of Christ's glorious work. The cross of Christ is a polyphonic accomplishment, an orchestra made up of many instruments playing different parts yet working in unison to compose a beautiful song that displays the manifold glory of the atonement and culminates in the chorus "Christ died for our sins!" As Bavinck says,

> The work of Christ is so multifaceted that it cannot be captured in a single word nor summarized in a single formula.

In the different books of the New Testament, therefore, different meanings of the death of Christ are highlighted, and all of them together help to give us a deep impression and a clear sense of the riches and many-sidedness of the mediator's work.[2]

Dimensions, Metaphors, and Theories

As mentioned in the introduction, I find "theories" to be an unhelpful category for the doctrine of atonement and prefer instead to focus on "dimensions" of the atonement. In fact, one of the goals of this book is to shift the conversation from exclusive *theories* to integrated *dimensions*. Before moving forward, though, I must briefly define my terms.

I understand a *dimension* of the atonement to refer to the reality (the thing itself) of what Christ accomplished through his saving work. A metaphor refers to the analogical language used from another sphere of life to further describe or illustrate a dimension. For example, justification draws from the legal sphere, propitiation from the cultic, and redemption from the marketplace. While there is a distinction between dimensions and metaphors, all language is metaphorical to a degree, and there is therefore an inevitable overlap of these two categories. *Theories* originated from the developing university system of the Enlightenment and refers to conceptually comprehensive (and therefore exclusive) explanations, usually centered on one dimension of the atonement.

For example, Romans 3:24 speaks of the "redemption that is in Christ Jesus." The dimension of *redemption* points to the fact that something happened on the cross where sinners are no longer slaves to their sin. The metaphor of redemption

---

2. Herman Bavinck, *Sin and Salvation in Christ*, vol. 3 of *Reformed Dogmatics*, ed. John Bolt, trans. John Vriend (Grand Rapids, MI: Baker Academic, 2003), 383.

appeals both to the exodus of Israel in the Old Testament and the slave market in the first-century world. An example of a theory would be a "ransom theory" that seeks to explain how freedom was purchased and to whom the price was paid.[3]

The Many Dimensions of Atonement

In the remainder of this chapter, we will survey twenty dimensions of Christ's atoning work. They are in no particular order, but in chapter 4 we will consider how to integrate the various dimensions. While these are brief overviews of each dimension, my hope is that as you read each one, your view of the atonement would expand and your heart would swell in praise for the glory of God in the cross of Christ.

Glorification

We were made for glory—created to receive and reflect the awe-inspiring wonder of God. Sin, however, turns our hunger for transcendence inward. Seeking glory for ourselves, we settle for the cheap substitute of fame. Jesus came to redirect our glory-starving hearts to the triune God, and he did so by going to the cross.

In the Gospel of John, Jesus repeatedly refers to the "hour" of glory that would be the apex of his mission (John 2:4; 4:21, 23; 5:25, 28; 7:30; 8:20). When Jesus enters Jerusalem on the week that he would be crucified, he tells his disciples, "The hour has come for the Son of Man to be glorified" (John 12:23). After discussing his upcoming death, Jesus says, "For this purpose I have come to this hour. Father, glorify your name" (John 12:27–28).

---

3. The theme of ransom raises two methodological points. First, metaphorical language is used to explain not only the outcome of atonement (redemption) but also the means (ransom). Second, the overlap of "redemption" and "ransom" should raise caution in too strictly dividing the means and the outcome. While I think it is helpful to make this distinction for heuristic reasons, we must remember that Christ's atoning death is an organically united work.

He then describes his ensuing death as being "lifted up" (John 12:32), showing that his crucifixion, while appearing as humiliation, was truly his glorification.

What does it mean that the cross is the hour of glory? That all depends on the definition of "glory." Glory is not merely beauty or excellence; it is the *display* of beauty and excellence. Glory is beauty beheld. The glory of God is God going public with his infinite praiseworthiness. The atoning death of Christ, therefore, is the place where God's glory shines brightest. It is not that God *became* more glorious through the cross. Rather, the cross is the place where his glory was made known and magnified to the uttermost.

The glory of God is the ultimate end of the atonement. And it is not only the Gospel of John that highlights this theme. The psalmist prays, "Atone for our sins, / for your name's sake" (Ps. 79:9). Paul says that "the rulers of this age . . . crucified the Lord of glory" (1 Cor. 2:8). According to the author of Hebrews, when Christ went to the cross he was "crowned with glory and honor because of the suffering of death" (Heb. 2:9). Revelation reveals myriads of angels praising the Lamb for his sacrificial suffering:

Worthy is the Lamb who was slain,
to receive power and wealth and wisdom and might
and honor and glory and blessing! (Rev. 5:12)[4]

Reconciliation

Broken relationships are one of the most agonizing parts of life. A disagreement with a friend or a falling out with a family member can bring tension into life that is almost unbearable. And the deeper the relationship, the more painful is the fracture.

4. For more depth on this theme of glorification through the cross, see Jeremy Treat, "The Glory of the Cross: How God's Power Is Made Perfect in Weakness," *Christianity Today* 57, no. 8 (October 2013): 56–59.

The plight of humanity is that while we were made to know God, we have become enemies instead of friends. Because of sin, hostility has replaced harmony, and tension has pervaded our entire relational world. But there is good news: "While we were enemies we were reconciled to God by the death of his Son" (Rom. 5:10). The word *reconciliation* comes from the realm of relationships and refers to the reuniting of two parties that were formerly alienated.

How, then, does Christ's death reconcile us to God? By dying in our place, Christ deals with our sin and its consequences, removing the barrier to fellowship. Yet the cross not only removes the barrier but also restores the relationship. The greatest good of the gospel is not forgiveness, victory, or redemption; rather it is God himself and his invitation to know him. As Paul says, "I count everything as loss because of the surpassing worth of knowing Christ Jesus my Lord" (Phil. 3:8). This restored relationship with God is not an undefined relationship. It is a covenant relationship. God has bound himself to his people by grace and declared over them, "I will be your God, and you shall be my people" (Jer. 7:23). As we will see in chapter 5, this vertical reconciliation leads to horizontal reconciliation. The reconciled become reconcilers in God's work of the reconciliation of the world.

Propitiation

According to Scripture, a core part of the human problem is that, apart from Christ, we are under the wrath of God because of our sin (Rom. 1:18). If God's holy response to sin is wrath, and we have all sinned, then the question is this: how can the wrath of God be removed? Does God simply change his mind about the wickedness of sin? Of course not. Does God merely dismiss our wrongdoing. No, for our God "will by no means clear the guilty" (Ex. 34:7).

The apostle Paul declares the good news against the backdrop of judgment and wrath: God put forward his Son "as a propitiation by his blood" (Rom. 3:25). The word *propitiation* refers to an act by which God becomes "propitious," or favorable, toward those who had sinned against him and were, therefore, under his wrath. The Greek word for propitiation is *hilastērion*, which is also the word used in the Greek translation of the Old Testament to describe the "mercy seat," the place on top of the ark of the covenant in the Holy of Holies where the blood of the sacrifice was sprinkled to atone for the sins of the people on the Day of Atonement.[5]

To say that Jesus is the propitiation for our sins means that the cross is the place where God's wrath is satisfied and his people's sins are forgiven. The wrath that was meant for us was borne by Jesus. Paul goes on to say that God put forward his Son as a propitiation "to show God's righteousness" (Rom. 3:25). Propitiation is the way that God can forgive sin while still upholding his righteousness. Only in this way can God be "just and the justifier" (Rom. 3:26).

While the word "propitiation" (*hilastērion*) is only used a few times, the concept of being delivered from the wrath of God is present throughout the New Testament (e.g., Rom. 5:9;

---

5. There are two common objections to propitiation. First, some argue that it is based on pagan understandings where people made sacrifices to appease the gods, particularly for crops, fertility, or battle. What is noteworthy of these pagan sacrifices is that humans made sacrifices to appease the gods. The biblical concept of propitiation, however, is God himself putting forth his Son as a sacrifice to be a propitiation for sins. It is not humans appeasing an irrationally angry god, but rather God bearing the consequences of our sin in order to reconcile us to himself. His wisdom made a way for his love to meet the demands of his justice. Propitiation is not something we do to pacify God but something God did to save us. Second, some argue that the "wrath of God" is simply a metaphorical way of talking about the inevitable consequences of sin and evil. However, beyond the fact that Scripture clearly speaks of God directly responding to sin, this position is also inconsistent. Should we speak of God's love as a metaphorical way of talking about the natural consequences of doing good? Of course not.

1 Thess. 1:10). And in the Old Testament, the forgiveness of sins is frequently paired with the removal of God's wrath (e.g., Ps. 85:2–3). As we have seen, God's wrath is not a whimsical display of rage but the measured enactment of his holy and just love. That is why 1 John 4:10 says, "In this is love, not that we have loved God but that he loved us and sent his Son to be the propitiation for our sins."

This brief overview of propitiation must be understood within a Trinitarian framework and still requires much nuance. D. A. Carson offers needed wisdom:

> When we use the language of propitiation, we are not to think that the Son, full of love, offered himself and thereby placated (i.e., rendered propitious) the Father, full of wrath. The picture is more complex. It is that the Father, full of righteous wrath against us, nevertheless loved us so much that he sent his Son. Perfectly mirroring his Father's words and deeds, the Son stood over against us in wrath—it is not for nothing that the Scriptures portray sinners wanting to hide from the face of him who sits on the throne *and from the wrath of the Lamb*—yet, obedient to his Father's commission, offered himself on the cross. He did this out of love both for his Father, whom he obeys, and for us, whom he redeems.[6]

As a pastor I often talk to Christians who assume that God is upset with them. Many followers of Jesus believe that their suffering must be a result of God punishing them for falling short. But the glorious truth of propitiation gives a different perspective. Jesus already took our judgment. Therefore, you can know that God is not angry with you nor is he punishing

---

6. D. A. Carson, *The Difficult Doctrine of the Love of God* (Wheaton, IL: Crossway, 2000), 72 (emphasis in original).

you. God is with you and for you. As the propitiation for sins (Rom. 3:25), Jesus bore the wrath that we deserve, thereby satisfying God's justice and expiating our sin.

Victory

Humanity was made to be sub-rulers in the kingdom of God, representing God's reign throughout the earth (Gen. 1:26–28). In our sin, however, we have rejected the King and been taken captive by the kingdom of darkness. Jesus is our victor who came to dethrone Satan, vanquish evil, and establish God's merciful and just kingdom on earth. "The reason the Son of God appeared was to destroy the works of the devil" (1 John 3:8). And he did so by going to the cross where he accomplished victory through surrender. The Son of God took on flesh so that "through death he might destroy the one who has the power of death, that is, the devil" (Heb. 2:14). By forgiving sin through Christ's death on the cross, God "disarmed the rulers and authorities and put them to open shame" (Col. 2:15).

These passages appeal to the conceptual world of warfare, presenting Christ as a conquering King who defeats his enemies in battle. Through the cross, the serpent has been defeated, put to shame, and stripped of his power of accusation over believers. Yet, while Christ is presented as a warrior King, he accomplishes victory in the most surprising way. By dealing with sin through sacrifice, Jesus disarms the enemy and reestablishes God's rightful authority. Christ is a conquering King. But he reigns with love, conquers through forgiveness, and brings the kingdom through the cross. As Athanasius says, "The cross of the Lord is the monument to his victory."[7]

---

7. Athanasius, *On the Incarnation*, trans. and ed. a Religious of C.S.M.V. (Crestwood, NY: St. Vladimir's Seminary Press, 2002), 60 (5.30).

Many Western Christians have neglected the victory dimension of the atonement because their post-enlightenment context does not take seriously the spiritual realm. We live in what Charles Taylor calls a "disenchanted world," where the primeval idea of spirits is only tolerated if relegated to private spirituality.[8] Globalization, however, is forcing the Western church to return to the Scriptures to rediscover the spiritually charged world we live in and how Christ is victorious over the powers. In a global city like Los Angeles, occultic activity has become mainstream in everyday spirituality. Whether praying to crystals, cleansing an apartment with sage, or looking to the stars for guidance, people are searching for a transcendent power in life. And it's not just Los Angeles. The fastest growing religion in the United States is witchcraft, with over one million practicing Wiccans (which means there are more practicing witches in the United States than there are Jehovah's Witnesses).[9] More than ever, we need to uphold Christ as our conquering King who has been given all authority in heaven and on earth.

Redemption

We were made to flourish under the reign of God, enjoying the freedom and peace of the kingdom. Because of our rebellion against God, however, we are slaves to sin, in bondage to the flesh, and under the oppression of the devil. Jesus is our liberator who came to set us free from the slavery of sin and to bring us into the freedom of his reign.

While redemption is a common theme in Scripture, Ephesians 1:7 succinctly puts it on display: "In him we have redemption through his blood." In the most basic sense, the word

---

8. Charles Taylor, *A Secular Age* (Cambridge, MA: Belknap, 2007), 41.
9. Tara Isabella Burton, *Strange Rites: New Religions for a Godless World* (New York: PublicAffairs, 2020), 117.

redeem means to set free (often by paying a price). Two different backgrounds inform the meaning of Christ's redemption: the exodus story where God sets his people free from slavery and the first-century slave market where a slave could be set free by the payment of a ransom price.

So what does it mean that Christ redeems sinners with his blood? First, through his death, Christ sets us free *from* the shackles of sin, the slavery of the flesh, and the power of the devil. Second, Christ not only frees us *from* sin and its consequences but also frees us *for* abundant life in his kingdom (Gal. 5:1). Christ's death accomplishes a new exodus in which God's people are ushered into the promised land of God's presence. Third, the redemption price, or ransom, is the blood of Christ. As Paul says, "There is one mediator between God and men, the man Christ Jesus, who gave himself as a ransom for all" (1 Tim. 2:5–6).

People long for freedom today. But "freedom" means something different in Western society than it does in the Scriptures. According to our culture, freedom is being able to do whatever you want. It is the removal of constraints and absence of authority. The problem with this version of freedom is that it ends up being another form of slavery—that is, slavery to your own desires. True freedom is not being able to do whatever you want; it is being able to do that for which you were made. Jesus is the only one who can set us free, redeeming us from our sin and for a life in his kingdom.

Justification

Imagine your life on trial in a cosmic courtroom. Your eternity hangs in the balance. Apart from the grace of Christ, God's verdict is clear and echoes throughout all of human history: "Guilty."

We have all transgressed God's law and deserve his justice. But God desires to reconcile us to himself and make all things right. Here is the dilemma: How can God justify his people and uphold his own just character? Surely for a judge to simply overlook guilt would be a miscarriage of injustice.

The Bible's solution to this dilemma is clear: "We have now been justified by his blood" (Rom. 5:9). Justification is a legal term. The opposite of being justified is to be condemned or declared guilty. To be justified means to be declared not guilty, or innocent.

How does Christ's death on the cross justify sinners before a holy God? Christ, who had no sin of his own, bears our guilt, takes our unrighteousness, and is condemned in our place. But we cannot stop there. Christ does not leave us in a place of innocent neutrality. We are declared righteous, yet it is not a righteousness of our own. Jesus lived a perfectly righteous life, always keeping the covenant and fulfilling the law in every way. Through his substitutionary death, we receive his righteousness (Rom. 5:19; 2 Cor. 5:21; Phil. 3:9). So when God looks at his justified people, he does not see our sin. He sees the righteousness of his Son.

The default mode of our fallen hearts is to try to earn our way into acceptance and approval. We try to justify ourselves through career, reputation, or accomplishments. But the attempt to earn righteousness nullifies the grace of God. For, as Paul says, "If righteousness were through the law, then Christ died for no purpose" (Gal. 2:21). Our self-justification projects reduce the cross to a relic, a backup plan for our otherwise performance-driven lives. Justification by faith, however, means that you do not earn your standing with God. You receive it. In Christ, the search for approval is over and the longing for acceptance is satisfied. We are justified by the blood of Jesus.

Sanctification

Sin is not merely a behavioral mistake with external consequences. Sin stains the soul and defiles us before a holy and
pure God (Ps. 106:39; Prov. 30:12; Mark 7:20). But thanks be
to God that Jesus is our sanctification (1 Cor. 1:30) and that
through his atoning death on the cross we are washed of our
sin and made holy and pure.

The author of Hebrews says, "Jesus also suffered outside
the gate in order to sanctify the people through his own blood"
(Heb. 13:12). To sanctify means to make holy, which entails
the removal or purification of that which is unholy. The Old
Testament background regarding the Day of Atonement makes
clear that sanctification comes through atonement: "For on this
day shall atonement be made for you to cleanse you. You shall
be clean before the LORD from all your sins" (Lev. 16:30). And
as the author of Hebrews argues, if the blood of goats purified
the defiled people in the Old Testament, then how much more
will the blood of Christ completely cleanse his people today
(Heb. 9:13–14)?

Those who trust in Christ are sanctified at conversion,
but there is still a process of living out that sanctification.[10]
Hebrews 10:14 says, "For by a single offering he has perfected
for all time those who are being sanctified." At regeneration,
the believer is completely washed of every stain and blemish.
The Christian life, then, is learning to be who you truly are, as
a sanctified child of God.

In Zechariah 3, the prophet has a vision of Joshua the high
priest standing before the Lord clothed with filthy garments.

---

10. In theology people often use justification to refer to conversion and sanctification for the progressive outworking of that conversion in a life of Christian growth.
While I am not against this approach in general, the Bible does not use "sanctification"
strictly in that sense. To sanctify means to cleanse, set apart, or make holy. Justification
is a forensic term, whereas sanctification is a cultic/moral term. Sanctification has an
already / not yet nature.

An angel declares, "Remove the filthy garments from him," and then says to Joshua, "Behold, I have taken your iniquity away from you, and I will clothe you with pure vestments" (Zech. 3:4). This is a picture of what the crucified Christ does for us. Our internal self is clothed in the filthy rags of injustice, idolatry, lust, pride, and coveting. But Christ takes our filthy rags on himself and clothes us with his holiness (Gal. 3:27). According to 1 John 1:7, "The blood of Jesus his Son cleanses us from all sin." Christ died for you "in order to present you holy and blameless and above reproach before him" (Col. 1:22).

Removal of Shame

Christians in Western cultures have vastly overlooked the way that Jesus dealt with our shame through his death. In the Bible, the term *guilt* and its various derivatives occur 155 times, whereas the term *shame* and its derivatives occur 345 times.[11] Yet theologians in the West give far greater attention to guilt than to shame.[12] We must recover the biblical truth that Christ bore our shame on the cross.

Jackson Wu offers a helpful definition: "Shame is the fear, pain, or state of being regarded unworthy of acceptance in social relationships."[13] Wu explains further by contrasting shame with guilt. "Guilt focuses on a person's actions or behavior. . . . Shame is more general and holistic. It focuses on a person's worth. Whereas guilt says, 'my actions were

---

11. Timothy C. Tennent, *Theology in the Context of World Christianity: How the Global Church Is Influencing the Way We Think about and Discuss Theology* (Grand Rapids, MI: Zondervan Academic, 2007), 92.

12. Tennent notes that the word *shame* does not even appear in the systematic theologies of Louis Berkhof, Wayne Grudem, W. G. T. Shedd, Wolfhart Pannenberg, Millard Erickson, or Helmut Thielicke. Tennent, *Theology in the Context of World Christianity*, 92.

13. Jackson Wu, "Have Theologians No Sense of Shame? How the Bible Reconciles Objective and Subjective Shame," *Themelios* 43, no. 2 (2018): 206.

bad,' shame instead says, 'I am bad.'"[14] A significant aspect of Wu's definition is that shame is about one's standing "in social relationships." Shame is inherently communal and focuses primarily on one's reputation or standing within the community. This explains why Western cultures often do not understand shame: it is hard to grasp an inherently communal idea within a highly individualized framework. Of course, the world of Scripture, far from an individualistic Western framework, was very much an honor/shame culture. In the New Testament, to shame (*kataischynō*) means to publicly humiliate or disgrace, whereas to honor (*timaō*) means to publicly acknowledge value.[15]

The themes of honor and shame are at the heart of the biblical narrative, particularly in relation to sin and salvation. Adam and Eve were originally naked and "were not ashamed" (Gen. 2:25), but their sin led to shame, shown in the narrative through the realization of their nakedness and their attempt to hide from God. Throughout the Scriptures, sin is defined (at least in part) as dishonoring God (Rom. 1:18–21), which results in a state of shame brought about by God's judgment (Dan. 12:2). For example, the Lord responds to Israel's sin by saying, "I will change their glory into shame" (Hos. 4:7). However, the Lord's salvation brings about a reversal of the effects of sin: "I will change their shame into praise and renown in all the earth" (Zeph. 3:19; cf. Rom. 10:11).

The reversal from shame to honor ultimately comes about through the crucifixion of the Son of God. Jesus himself spoke of his ensuing death in terms of shame (Luke 18:32–33) but

---

14. Wu, "Have Theologians No Sense of Shame?," 206. Wu also corrects a common misconception, arguing that shame does in fact have objective and subjective expressions.

15. Walter Bauer, *A Greek-English Lexicon of the New Testament and Other Early Christian Literature*, rev. and ed. Frederick William Gingrich, 3rd ed. (Chicago: University of Chicago Press, 2000), s.v. "καταισχύνω" and "τιμάω."

with the end goal being honor and glorification (John 17:1–5; Phil. 2:9–11). The crucifixion account is told in the Gospels in such a way that puts shame at the center of the story. Jesus was stripped naked (an indicator of bearing Adam's shame from the garden of Eden) and mocked as a pretender king. The cross was not merely punishment for a guilty verdict; it was public humiliation meant to devalue the personhood of Jesus and smear his reputation. Yet, as the Gospels make clear, he who was lifted up in mockery was truly being enthroned in honor and glory.

The author of Hebrews beautifully displays the honor and shame framework for the death of Christ. By suffering in our place, Jesus "endured the cross, despising the shame" (Heb. 12:2). But, through bearing our shame, he was truly being "crowned with glory and honor because of the suffering of death" (Heb. 2:9). Furthermore, his death was for the purpose of "bringing many sons to glory" (Heb. 2:10). In a wondrous exchange, Jesus bore our shame so that we could receive his honor.

New Covenant

Christ died to reconcile sinners into a relationship with their Creator, but it is not a generic, undefined relationship. Rather, Christ's atoning work reconciles sinners into a *covenant* relationship with God. Reconciliation has always been the aim of atonement, but reconciliation in Scripture has a covenantal ring.

A covenant in Scripture is a binding agreement, based on vows, that makes two parties one family. That is how the word *covenant* is used when we talk about marriage (a covenant relationship), and that is how God uses the word with his people. The Lord binds himself to his beloved by grace.

Throughout Scripture, covenants are often sealed with sacrifice.[16] When God makes a covenant with Abram, there is a ceremony involving sacrifice, symbolizing that if the covenant is broken, God himself will bear the curse (Gen. 15:1–17; cf. Jer. 34:18). When God makes a covenant with Israel after the exodus, Moses ratifies the covenant with the blood of sacrifice (Ex. 24:1–7). At the Last Supper, Jesus reimagines the exodus tradition around himself as the Passover lamb: "This is my blood of the covenant, which is poured out for many for the forgiveness of sins" (Matt. 26:28). As the old covenant was inaugurated by blood, Christ's sacrificial death seals the new covenant between God and his people (Heb. 10:15–22). Jesus is "our Passover lamb" (1 Cor. 5:7) who brings about a new exodus and a new covenant.

Covenant is essential for understanding the atoning significance of Christ's death for at least three reasons. First, Christ's death must be understood as a covenantal sacrifice, meaning that it atoned for sins and served to remind the covenant parties of the consequences for breaking the covenant, thereby calling for faithfulness. Second, in his death, Christ does not merely bear any penalty; rather, he bears the covenant curses, which include refusal of forgiveness and the bestowal of God's anger (Deut. 29:20–21). Third, by bearing the curses of the covenant through his sacrificial death, Jesus ratifies the new covenant. In sum, Christ fulfills the covenant obligations with his life, bears the covenant sanctions through his sacrificial death, and reconciles God and sinners into a covenant relationship.[17]

---

16. O. Palmer Robertson succinctly defines a covenant as "a bond in blood sovereignly administered" in *The Christ of the Covenants* (Grand Rapids, MI: Baker, 1980), 4.

17. To further explore this theme, see Jeremy Treat, "Atonement and Covenant: Binding Together Aspects of Christ's Work," in *Locating Atonement: Explorations in Constructive Dogmatics*, ed. Oliver Crisp and Fred Sanders (Grand Rapids, MI: Zondervan Academic, 2015), 101–17.

Revelation

What is God like? At the most basic level, the Christian's answer is simply "Jesus." He is "the image of the invisible God" (Col. 1:15) and "the exact imprint of his nature" (Heb. 1:3). Going a step further, the pinnacle of God's self-revelation is the crucifixion of the eternal Son. The cross is a window into the heart of God.

The cross reveals God's love through the forgiveness of sin, God's justice through the judgment of sin, God's power through the triumph over the devil, and God's wisdom in the way he saves sinners by grace. The cross is the ultimate "thus sayeth the Lord," revealing the majesty of God's character and the beauty of his plan.

A true understanding of Christ crucified leads not merely to a theology *about* the cross but a theology *of* the cross. In other words, the cross is the lens through which we understand all theology. Martin Luther compared the theology of the cross to a theology of (worldly) glory.[18] A theology of worldly glory expects to know God based on worldly standards. If worldly strength is demonstrated in raw power, one would expect the same of God. If worldly victory comes through force, one would expect the same of God. But the self-giving death of Christ reveals that God does not operate by the ways of the world. The cross is a billboard to the world declaring God's heart for sinners and his plan to renew creation.

When people experience trials in life they often wonder whether God cares. How can we know that God is good and is for us? For the Christian, we have an assurance of God's character by looking not to our circumstances but to Christ's cross. For it is at the cross where God reveals his undying love for us.

18. For a helpful overview of Luther's theology of the cross, see Gerhard Forde, *On Being a Theologian of the Cross: Reflections on Luther's Heidelberg Disputation, 1518* (Grand Rapids, MI: Eerdmans, 1997).

Return from Exile

In the garden of Eden, Adam and Eve were at home with their Maker. They experienced safety, intimacy, and love with God and one another. But when our first parents ate the fruit and sinned against God, they were banished from the garden, experiencing physical displacement and holistic dissonance as a result of living outside of God's gracious reign. The biblical word for this experience is *exile*. Ever since that day, all of humanity has been in exile.

Of course, the exile of Israel was one of the low points in the history of God's people. Babylon burned the temple, decimated Jerusalem, and dragged God's people hundreds of miles away from home. After seventy years of exile, God's people finally returned home. Yet even though Israel was back in the promised land, they had an ongoing sense that they remained in exile. The Old Testament ends with partial fulfillment of God's promises but an even greater longing to be at home with the Lord once again.

Just as Nehemiah left his comfortable position in the palace to restore the city of Jerusalem, Jesus left his throne in heaven and entered exile to restore the kingdom of God. Jesus suffered and died as an outcast "outside the gate" (Heb. 13:12) to bring us into the family of God. He is the "beloved son" who is thrown "out of the vineyard and killed" (Luke 20:13–15) as part of God's plan to restore Eden. Christ entered into exile so that we may be at home with the Lord. But while we are citizens of heaven, we are still sojourners and exiles on earth (1 Pet. 1:1). We are not home yet.

Adoption

Apart from Christ, we are spiritual orphans who have chosen insecurity and oppression over the strong and tender care of our heavenly Father. But God does not leave us to our own ruin. In an unthinkable act, God adopts sinners into his family through the blood of Christ. Paul says, "But when the fullness of time had come, God sent forth his Son, born of woman, born under the law, to redeem those who were under the law, so that we might receive adoption as sons" (Gal. 4:4–5). We were rebels who have been made sons and daughters and given a place at the table.

While the imagery of an infant being adopted is a powerful picture of God's redeeming grace, the typical Roman practice in the first century was to adopt adults, primarily for the purpose of passing on an inheritance. For example, a man of wealth with no children would legally adopt one of his slaves to pass on his inheritance. The slave not only became a son but an heir. Hence, Paul says, "So you are no longer a slave, but a son, and if a son, then an heir through God" (Gal. 4:7). When the slave becomes a son, all the status, rights, and inheritance of the family immediately belong to him.

Being adopted into the family of God is grounded in Christ's atoning work. What Paul says about adoption in Galatians 4 is an implication of what he declared in Galatians 3 about atonement. "Christ redeemed us from the curse of the law by becoming a curse for us—for it is written, 'Cursed is everyone who is hanged on a tree'—so that in Christ Jesus the blessing of Abraham might come to the Gentiles, so that we might receive the promised Spirit through faith" (Gal. 3:13–14). Christ's substitutionary death brings about the fulfillment of God's promise to Abraham to make a family of many nations. Through the cross, we are adopted into a family that is bound together not by DNA but by the blood of Christ.

The good news of adoption in Christ compels the church to be an adoptive people. Because we too were orphans, our hearts break for orphans. Because we have been transformed by adoptive grace, we seek to extend adoptive grace. When I see the joy and gratitude on the faces of children in our church who have been adopted or are in foster care, I'm reminded of the good news that we were orphans who have been brought in by God.

Apocalypse

The cross is the end of the world. And the beginning of a new one. In other words, the cross is apocalyptic, bringing about the eschatological turn of the ages in the world's redemptive historical timeline.

The Gospels show the apocalyptic nature of the cross by recounting the many signs of the end times that take place during the crucifixion of Christ. The sky goes dark (Matt. 27:45). The earth quakes (Matt. 27:51). The dead rise (Matt. 27:52). The temple veil is torn (Matt. 27:51). And a Gentile declares Jesus to be the Son of God (Matt. 27:54). The cross brings the end times into the middle of history, initiating a new era of what will culminate in the eternal kingdom of God.

The apostle Paul also sees the cross through an apocalyptic lens. In Galatians 1:4, he declares that Jesus "gave himself for our sins to deliver us from the present evil age" (Gal. 1:4). In other words, the atoning death of Jesus not only deals with our wickedness but also delivers us from the wickedness that characterizes this age. Paul goes on in Galatians 6:14–16 to assert that the cross is essential for the eschatological new creation. Through the cross, a new age breaks in—an era characterized not by the depravity of mankind but by the redeeming grace of God. And while there is certainly an overlap of the ages, the death of Jesus is the pivot point from "the present evil age" (Gal. 1:4) to "the age to come" (Heb. 6:5). Christ's atoning death is the causative turning point from the broken creation to the new creation.

Hebrews 9:26 says that Christ "has appeared once for all at the end of the ages to put away sin by the sacrifice of himself." By atoning for humanity's sin, God reconciles his people to himself and establishes his reign on earth as it is in heaven. The cross, therefore, is the climactic midpoint of redemptive history, the hinge on which the ages turn. In other words, Christ's death "for our sins" delivers us from the "evil age" and thereby brings about the new age of God's reign.

Healing

Sin brings death in its wake (Rom. 5:12). Because of sin, we live in a world with chemotherapy, breathing tubes, and ambulances. Furthermore, sickness and injury are not one-off instances in an otherwise healthy world. All of creation is groaning in the pain and brokenness of the fall (Rom. 8:22–23). But in a world under the decay of sin, the prophet Isaiah spoke of a Messiah who would provide a remedy: "With his wounds we are healed" (Isa. 53:5).

Matthew tells of Jesus healing the sick (Matt. 8:16) and then says, "This was to fulfill what was spoken by the prophet Isaiah: 'He took our illnesses and bore our diseases'" (Matt. 8:17). It is noteworthy that Matthew sees this prophecy being fulfilled in the life of Christ. We should not draw a line, however, between Christ's life and death. The healings, miracles, and exorcisms of Jesus were all miniature in-breakings of the kingdom of God—a kingdom that would be established through the cross and consummated at the return of Christ. How does Jesus bring about ultimate healing for his people? Christ conquered disease and death by taking them onto himself and suffering in the stead of his people. He suffered and died so that we might live and flourish.

The mission of Christ brings spiritual *and* physical healing. A key insight in the Gospels, however, is how these two are often connected. In Mark 2, a paralytic comes to Jesus for physical healing, but Jesus addresses his physical and spiritual condition: "Your sins are forgiven. . . . Rise, take up your bed and walk" (Mark 2:5, 9). The healing of Jesus extends from the soul to the body.

Healing must be understood within the "already" and "not yet" of the kingdom of God. Because the kingdom has already come, we should expect to experience some healing in this life. But because the kingdom has not yet been consummated, we should not expect to see the fullness of healing in this life. God can be glorified through miraculous healing and through faithful suffering.

Christ has already accomplished all that is necessary for the full healing of his people. One day we will have resurrection bodies in a new creation. But until that day, we pray for healing and wait with faith-filled anticipation. For our hope is this: Christ will return, and "he will wipe away every tear from their eyes, and death shall be no more, neither shall there be mourning, nor crying, nor pain anymore" (Rev. 21:4).

Temple

In the Old Testament, the temple was (1) the dwelling place for the holy God and (2) the place of atonement for unholy people. The entire purpose of the temple was for God to be able to dwell with his people, and at the heart of this vision was substitutionary atonement.

In the New Testament, the temple plays a crucial role for interpreting the death of Christ. When Jesus first enters Jerusalem, he curses the temple and declares that he will build it anew in three days, referring to his own bodily resurrection (John 2:19–22). And then, after Jesus breathed his last on the cross, the curtain within the temple was torn from top to bottom (Matt. 27:50–51), symbolizing the destruction of the temple and the unleashing of God's presence.

The crucified and resurrected Christ is the new temple. When Israel wanted to be in the presence of God and cleansed of their sin, they went to the temple. Now, we go to Jesus. Christ is the dwelling place of God and the place of atonement for sinners. His death nullified the sacrificial system in the temple, and his resurrected body is the new temple.

The temple was the axis point between heaven and earth. But on the cross, Jesus brought heaven and earth together so that the holy God could dwell with his redeemed people. For this reason, there will be no temple in the new creation, for God will dwell with his people in a renewed world, unhindered by sin (Rev. 21:22). In fact, when the book of Revelation tells of the New Jerusalem descending on the earth, it describes the dimensions of the city as a perfect cube (Rev. 21:16), echoing the dimensions of the Holy of Holies. Through the sacrificial death of Christ, all of creation will be the Holy of Holies, where the holy God will dwell with his purified people.

Example

The death of Jesus provides not only the pardon for our sin but also the pattern for our lives. Peter told the dispersed exiles, "For to this you have been called, because Christ also suffered for you, leaving you an example, so that you might follow in his steps" (1 Pet. 2:21). The cross creates a cruciform people who follow in the path of the servant King. [19]

Unfortunately, the subjective dimensions of the atonement (its ongoing effects on our lives) have often been pitted against the objective (what Christ accomplished definitively in reconciling people to God). Yet the objective and subjective dimensions of atonement not only need to be upheld but also properly ordered. For if Christ is our example without being our Savior, then he would only be an unattainable standard. We would have the pattern without the power.

There are at least three ways that the objective and subjective aspects of the atonement relate. First, the objective is the foundation for the subjective. We cannot follow Jesus's example without being changed by his accomplishment. Furthermore, Christ's atonement is aimed at both objective and subjective achievements. The forgiveness of our sin and the formation of our character are both benefits of the cross. The subjective is guaranteed by the objective, and the objective inherently flows into the subjective. We can only live by his example if we have been renewed by his death.

Second, the Holy Spirit is the power needed to follow in Jesus's steps. The love demonstrated at the cross is poured into our hearts by the Holy Spirit for the purpose of making us a cruciform people (Rom. 5:5). God's promise in the new covenant is "I will put my Spirit within you, and cause you to walk in my statutes" (Ezek. 36:27). A proper view of the exemplary dimension of Christ's atonement will be paired with an understanding of the way that sinners are united with

---

19. Does substitutionary atonement encourage oppressed people to remain in oppressive circumstances? Quite the opposite. While the cross is a model of faithful suffering, it is also the means by which Christ exposes injustice and breaks the chains of oppression. Furthermore, the cross is the revelation of God's justice against all sin, including oppression and injustice. The cross creates a redeemed people who know how to suffer faithfully and participate in God's work of setting the oppressed free.

Christ by the Spirit. To imitate Christ, we must abide in him by the Spirit.

Third, the exemplary dimension of Christ's atonement does include objective aspects as well. Through his accomplishment, Christ *revealed* God's love and *provided* an example of faithful suffering for God's purposes.

In sum, Christ is our example. But while the exemplary dimension of the atonement is not incorrect, it is insufficient if not joined to the objective aspects of Christ's work. Jesus is a Savior before he is an example. And we can only follow in his steps if we have been changed by his death and filled with his Spirit. As Miroslav Volf says, "The cross will serve best as the model if it has first served as the *foundation*."[20]

Forgiveness

Because of our sin, we are in debt to God (Matt. 6:12) and are guilty before God (James 2:10). But at the heart of the good news is the declaration that God forgives our sins on the basis of Christ's atoning work. And while atonement is about more than the forgiveness of sins, it is certainly not about less.[21]

Forgiveness is not merely dismissing a wrong. My wife and I teach our children that when someone apologizes to them, they should not respond by simply saying, "It's okay" (because whatever the offense is, it is not okay). To truly forgive, one acknowledges the wrongdoing but chooses to not hold it against the wrongdoer. Forgiveness is not merely dismissing a wrong; it is accepting the penalty on behalf of the wrongdoer for the sake of the relationship. It is absorbing the pain yourself rather than seeking to put it back on the other person. This is what Christ

---

20. Miroslav Volf, *Exclusion and Embrace: A Theological Exploration of Identity, Otherness, and Reconciliation* (Nashville: Abingdon, 1996), 22 (emphasis in original).
21. The concept of forgiveness includes many different Hebrew and Greek words that can mean to separate, cancel, cover, and so on.

has done for us on the cross. Jesus did not shrug his shoulders at our sin and say, "It's okay." He sees our sin for what it is—rebellion against God that deserves death. Jesus offers forgiveness, and he does so by bearing the pain himself.

The Old Testament especially demonstrates how atonement is the basis for the forgiveness of sins. The book of Leviticus, for example, uses a common formula for atonement and forgiveness: "The priest shall make atonement for him for his sin, and he shall be forgiven" (Lev. 4:26). This carries through to the New Testament with the clear connection between Christ's blood and forgiveness: "This is my blood of the covenant, which is poured out for many for the forgiveness of sins" (Matt. 26:28). "In him we have redemption through his blood, the forgiveness of our trespasses" (Eph. 1:7). "Without the shedding of blood there is no forgiveness of sins" (Heb. 9:22).

Forgiveness of sins must not only be understood in an individual sense but also in a communal sense. For Isaiah, in particular, the new exodus entails the corporate forgiveness of God's people (Isa. 40:2; 43:25; 44:22; cf. 33:24), echoing the great revelation of the God who is "merciful and gracious . . . forgiving iniquity and transgression and sin" (Ex. 34:6–7). Forgiveness reminds us of the gift of grace but also the cost of grace. Our debt is forgiven because Jesus paid it with his blood. Our guilt is removed because Jesus bore it on the cross.

Theosis

The greatest benefit of the gospel is God himself. To be more specific, through the blood of Christ, we are invited to participate in the life of the triune God. As Scripture says, "He has granted to us his precious and very great promises, so that through them you may become partakers of the divine nature" (2 Pet. 1:4). While many Protestants are apprehensive about the language of participation (and particularly Eastern Orthodox views of theosis or deification), we must take seriously the biblical claim of being partakers of the divine nature and being one with God (1 Cor. 6:17).[22]

Athanasius represents the early church's thinking about theosis, making the following well-known claim about Christ: "He, indeed, assumed humanity that we might become God."[23] Athanasius does not mean that humanity ceases to be human, nor does he obliterate a distinction between the Creator and creatures. Rather, he is referring to communion with the persons of the Trinity as the apex of salvation. He explains the Trinitarian logic of participation in his *Contra Arianos*,

> For since the Word is in the Father, and the Spirit is given from the Word, he wills that we should receive the Spirit, that when we receive it, thus having the Spirit of the Word which is in the Father, we too may be found, on account of the Spirit, to become one in the Word, and through him in the Father.[24]

Khaled Anatolios builds on Athanasius's work and argues that humanity was made to participate in the life of the triune God. And while our sin has separated us from God, Anatolios sees "salvation as a reintegration into mutual trinitarian glorification."[25] How does Christ accomplish such a salva-

---

22. Robert Letham explains why some Christians have been suspicious of theosis: "Reformed commentators have frequently considered theosis to entail the pagan notion of apotheosis, humanity being elevated to divine status, undergoing ontological change. Such an idea would carry with it an inevitable blurring of the Creator-creature distinction, foundational to the whole of biblical revelation." Robert Letham, *Union with Christ: In Scripture, History, and Theology* (Phillipsburg, NJ: P&R, 2011), 91.

23. Athanasius, *On the Incarnation*, 93 (8.54).

24. Athanasius, *Four Discourses against the Arians*, in *Athanasius: Selected Works*, vol. 4 of *Nicene and Post-Nicene Fathers*, Series 2, ed. Philip Schaff and Henry Wace (Peabody, MA: Hendrickson, 2012), 407 (3.25).

25. Khaled Anatolios, *Deification through the Cross: An Eastern Christian Theology of Salvation* (Grand Rapids, MI: Eerdmans, 2020), 376.

tion? Anatolios summarizes his view as *deification through the cross.* By crucifixion, Jesus pays the penalty for human sin and glorifies the Father. His death opens up the divine life to sinners.

An emphasis on union with God is not confined to the early church or Eastern Orthodoxy. Medieval mystics such as John of the Cross and Teresa of Avila saw the goal of life as the union of our souls with God through love. The Reformer John Calvin says, "We shall be partakers of divine and blessed immortality and glory, so as to be as it were one with God as far as our capacities will allow."[26]

Immortality

God created humanity for abundant and immortal life. That is why God warned that the penalty of sin would be nothing short of death (Gen. 2:17). Of course, humanity sinned and, therefore, deserves this penalty. But God, in his love, sought to rescue humanity from its corruption and death. The divine dilemma, however, was that God is immortal and could not die. Athanasius describes how the incarnation is the solution:

> The Word perceived that corruption could not be got rid of otherwise than through death; yet He Himself, as the Word, being immortal and the Father's Son, was such as could not die. For this reason, therefore, He assumed a body capable of death, in order that it, through belonging to the Word Who is above all, might become in dying a sufficient exchange for all, and, itself remaining incorruptible through

---

26. John Calvin, *Commentary on the Catholic Epistles,* trans. and ed. John Owen (repr., Grand Rapids, MI: Baker, 1996), 371. Of course, there are differences in Calvin's view and that of Eastern Orthodoxy or the early church. See J. Todd Billings, "United to God through Christ: Assessing Calvin on the Question of Deification," *Harvard Theological Review* 98, no. 3 (2005): 315–34.

His indwelling, might thereafter put an end to corruption for all other as well, by the grace of the resurrection.[27]

In other words, while God desired to share his incorruptibility with his creatures, sin led humanity into corruption and decay. But God became man; the incorruptible took on corruption so that we might share in the incorruptibility of God.

Athanasisus goes on to quote Hebrews 2:14–15, which declares that Jesus conquers death through death. How is this possible? First, death is the penalty for sin, and Jesus bore our penalty in our place, thereby nullifying the sentence of death for us. He disarms Satan of his power of accusation and removes the fear of death because the resurrection transforms death from a grave into a doorway. Second, by entering into death as the God-man, he negates the very essence of death. Benjamin Myers explains: "Swallowing a human body, death discovers that it has also swallowed God. Because of the union of natures in Christ, it is possible for the impassible divine nature to enter death and to overcome it from within."[28]

Christ died so that we could live. He "abolished death and brought life and immortality to light through the gospel" (2 Tim. 1:10). And while we still experience pain, corruption, and physical death as we wait for the return of Christ, we can look forward with hope to the day when "death shall be no more" (Rev. 21:4).

Shalom

Shalom is a Hebrew word that captures the scope of God's vision for creation and redemption. While it is often trans-

---

27. Athanasius, *On the Incarnation*, 35 (2.9).
28. Benjamin Myers, "The Patristic Atonement Model," in Crisp and Sanders, *Locating Atonement*, 76.

lated in English as "peace," the Hebrew concept means much more than the absence of war or a calm psychological state. In the Scriptures, shalom has a positive meaning, referring to the goodness of God's creation functioning in harmony and wholeness. Shalom is the experience of the fullness of God's blessing where all creation is working together for his glory and our good. In other words, shalom is simply how the world is meant to be under the loving reign of God. Sin, however, is "the vandalism of shalom."[29] Our rebellion against God exchanges peace with hostility, fracturing the goodness of humanity's relationship with God, one another, and creation.

Jesus, however, came on a mission to restore shalom. Jesus is our peace (Eph. 2:14), makes peace (Eph. 2:15–16), and proclaims peace (Eph. 2:17).[30] But how does Jesus bring about peace? He is reconciling all things through "making peace by the blood of his cross" (Col. 1:20). Jesus fulfills the prophecy of the suffering servant: "Upon him was the chastisement that brought us peace [*shalom*]" (Isa. 53:5). As Graham Cole says, "Atonement brings shalom by defeating the enemies of peace, overcoming the barriers both to reconciliation and to the restoration of creation. This is God the peacemaker's mission."[31]

More Dimensions to Explore

My hope is that surveying twenty dimensions of Christ's atoning work explodes the standard approach of three mutually exclusive theories and invites people to explore the depths of

---

29. Cornelius Plantinga, *Not the Way It's Supposed to Be: A Breviary of Sin* (Grand Rapids, MI: Eerdmans, 1995), 7.

30. The Hebrew word *shalom* is often rendered in the Greek translation of the Old Testament as *eirēnē* and carries similar connotations.

31. Graham Cole, *God the Peacemaker: How Atonement Brings Shalom*, New Studies in Biblical Theology 25 (Downers Grove, IL: IVP Academic, 2009), 229.

God's manifold wisdom in Christ. Furthermore, while these twenty dimensions are meant to stretch one's view of the cross, this is certainly not an exhaustive list. Below is a sampling of further dimensions of Christ's work that could be explored for an even more holistic approach to the doctrine of atonement. Scripture presents Christ's death as . . .

- a husband laying down his life for his wife (Eph. 5:25);
- a seed planted in the ground that bears fruit (John 12:23–34);
- a ratification of a will (Heb. 9:17);
- a friend who lays down his life for his friends (John 15);
- a shepherd laying down his life for the sheep (John 10:15);
- the bronze serpent lifted up in the wilderness (John 3:14);
- the stone that the builders rejected but has become the cornerstone (Mark 11:10);
- the donation of riches (2 Cor. 8:9);
- childbirth (John 16:21);
- exaltation (John 12:32).

A Remedy for Every Disease

The multidimensional nature of the atonement has significant practical and pastoral implications. Our comprehensive brokenness demands a comprehensive renewal. And each dimension of the atonement can be applied to one's particular situation. A person being oppressed by the demonic does not primarily need to hear about justification but rather that Christ is our conquering King who reigns over us with peace. Someone struggling with shame does not need to hear about propitiation as much as the fact that Christ has borne our shame. A person riddled with guilt over sin does not need to have Christ highlighted as our example but rather as the one who has taken away our condemnation. The doctrine of atonement is like a medicine cabinet for weary souls. And we need all the dimensions of Christ's work to experience his kingdom on earth as it is in heaven. "For from his fullness we have all received, grace upon grace" (John 1:16).

4

The Coherence of Atonement

An Integrated Accomplishment

In him all things hold together.
COLOSSIANS 1:17

The process of reconciliation started by Christ
includes the hope of a renewed creation and
of the reconciliation to God of all things.[1]
SANYU IRALU

Jesus's death on the cross is a many-splendored accomplishment, confronting the complexity of our sinful disease with the manifold remedy of God's grace. But it is not enough to stop at the multidimensionality of the atonement. We must move from complexity to coherence.

---

1. Sanyu Iralu, "Colossians," in *South Asia Bible Commentary*, ed. Brian Wintle (Grand Rapids, MI: Zondervan, 2015), 1662.

The Danger of Disconnected Plurality

In the last chapter we discussed the danger of one-dimensional reductionism—namely, truncating Christ's glorious work to only one aspect of it, like picking a ray of light and calling it the sun. I corrected this error by highlighting numerous dimensions of the atonement. There is an opposite error, however, that we also must beware of: disconnected plurality. This approach appreciates the diversity of dimensions of the atonement but simply upholds all the dimensions with no integration or balance, often reducing the array of dimensions to mere synonyms or alternative options to be chosen based on preference or context.

The danger of interpreting the dimensions as mere synonyms (different ways of saying the same thing) is that it flattens out the multiplicity of the atonement, minimizing the unique contribution of each dimension. This also shifts the weight of diversity from Christ's objective accomplishment to our subjective understanding of it, from theology to epistemology. A better approach is to acknowledge that Christ's accomplishment *is* multifaceted and is *revealed* in diverse ways as well. The dimensions of the atonement are not mere synonyms but are each unique contributions to a beautifully variegated accomplishment. The various aspects of the atonement are not interchangeable but are complementary.

Reducing the dimensions of atonement to alternative options also diminishes the glory of the cross. This relativistic pick-your-dimension approach fails to appreciate how Christ solves the holistic problem of humanity as opposed to simply providing an assortment of remedies here or there. In other words, the atonement is less like a buffet and more like a well-rounded diet. While the various dimensions certainly apply to different contexts (as noted at the end of the last chapter), each dimension is an entry point to a greater whole, not an alternative based on preference.

In sum, we need to avoid one-dimensional reductionism (narrowing Christ's atoning work to one dimension or theory) and disconnected plurality (upholding the many dimensions without discerning how they relate to one another). My aim, therefore, is to construct an integrated and balanced approach to the multidimensional work of Christ.[2] The various dimensions of the atonement are not merely to be upheld in a state of coexistence; they must fit together into a coherent whole.

An Integrated and Balanced Approach

The various dimensions of the atonement should not compete against one another but complement one another as mutually enriching aspects of Christ's work. Hans Urs von Balthasar offers three helpful warnings about the way the various aspects should relate to one another. First, no aspect must be allowed to dominate and so diminish the significance of the others. Second, no aspect can replace the center to which it points. Third, the tension between the aspects cannot be slackened for the sake of synthesis but must be endured. As Balthasar says, "One sided approaches . . . infallibly result in a loss of theo-dramatic tension in the whole."[3]

To go a step further, the goal is not merely to uphold tension but to move toward integration. This is the way of Scripture itself. As Karl Barth says, "The different groups of terms cut across each other very frequently."[4] Fleming Rutledge adds, "The

---

2. My goal is not to integrate the various dimensions into a comprehensive *theory*. As previously mentioned, I do not believe that constructing theories is the way forward in the doctrine of atonement. My aim, rather, is to show how integration needs to permeate our approach to the atonement in general. I am using the story of the kingdom as *an* integrating framework, with substitution as its center, but I am not claiming it is *the* framework for atonement.

3. Hans Urs von Balthasar, *The Action*, vol. 4 of *Theo-Drama: Theological Dramatic Theory*, trans. Graham Harrison (San Francisco: Ignatius, 1994), 244.

4. Karl Barth, *The Doctrine of Reconciliation*, vol. 4/1 of *Church Dogmatics*, ed. G. W. Bromiley and Thomas Torrance, trans. G. W. Bromiley (Edinburgh: T&T Clark, 1958), 274.

images often overlap and interpret one another."[5] And John Stott sums it up well when he says, "They are not alternative explanations of the cross, providing us with a range to choose from, but complementary to one another, each contributing a vital part to the whole."[6]

An important part of integration is balance. It is possible to affirm the comprehensiveness of Christ's work but functionally reduce it to one part. For example, many liberal theologians have largely neglected the biblical theme of the wrath of God in relation to the atonement. Many conservative theologians have ignored the biblical theme of Satan's dominion. Both sides, at least in an American context, have overlooked the important place of shame in Christ's work. We must seek to uphold the many dimensions of Christ's work and do so with integration and balance.[7]

It is not enough to be comprehensive without also having coherence. That is why our approach must be less like a shotgun (with a variety of dimensions blasted out) and more like a spiderweb (where every dimension is connected to and dependent on the rest). Otherwise, one aspect of the truth becomes diminished and even distorted when not held in relation to other aspects of the truth.

Josh McNall compares the atonement to a mosaic, where each dimension fits together to form a picture of Christ that

---

5. Fleming Rutledge, *The Crucifixion: Understanding the Death of Jesus Christ* (Grand Rapids, MI: Eerdmans, 2015), 208.

6. John Stott, *The Cross of Christ* (Downers Grove, IL: InterVarsity Press, 1986), 168.

7. Balance includes, at some level, proper proportions as well. Of course, we are not expected to give equal treatment to every dimension of the atonement. Henri Blocher lays out the following criteria for how to determine the proportions of attention given to each dimension: (1) frequency: regularity, development, and relation to other metaphors; (2) linguistic intentionality: how literally the author intends to use the metaphor; (3) genre: the more didactic genres offer greater conceptual clarity. Henri Blocher, "Biblical Metaphors and the Doctrine of the Atonement," *Journal of the Evangelical Theological Society* 47 (2004): 639.

leads to adoration.[8] We cannot merely lay the pieces of Christ's work on the table and leave them unconnected. Rather, every piece must fit with the others and play its part in contributing to the whole. According to McNall, "Mosaics show us how the pieces fit together while also allowing each piece to retain a recognizable particularity."[9] The various dimensions of Christ's work hold together, providing a comprehensive picture of the atonement that leads to worship.

While integration is the focus of this chapter, I have not waited until now to begin this important work. Thus far, I have given a framework (the biblical story of the kingdom of God) and a center (Christ's death in our place and for our sins). A center and a framework help orient every dimension to the story and to one other. Furthermore, I have integrated other doctrines into the atonement (e.g., the Trinity, Christology, hamartiology, eschatology). And lastly, many of the dimensions that I have worked with are integrative in and of themselves. For example, adoption integrates legal and familial conceptual worlds, while covenant is deeply personal yet formally legal.

Why should we seek integration in the doctrine of atonement? As we will see in the rest of this chapter, the dimensions of the atonement are integrated in Scripture, have been integrated throughout church history, and therefore should be integrated in theology today.

Integration in Scripture

It will not do to simply catalog the various dimensions of atonement and uphold the tension. Why? Because Scripture

---

8. Joshua M. McNall, *The Mosaic of Atonement: An Integrated Approach to Christ's Work* (Grand Rapids, MI: Zondervan Academic, 2019).

9. McNall, *The Mosaic of Atonement,* 21.

itself interweaves and overlaps the various dimensions. The following three passages are examples of how the authors of Scripture mix metaphors and integrate various dimensions of the atonement.

Romans 3:23–25

In Romans 3:23–25, Paul uses three different metaphors from three different realms of society to explain the meaning of Christ's death. But again, he is not saying the same thing in three different ways. He is drawing from different conceptual worlds to explain different yet mutually enriching dimensions of what Christ accomplished:

> For all have sinned and fall short of the glory of God, and are justified [law court] by his grace as a gift, through the redemption [marketplace] that is in Christ Jesus, whom God put forward as a propitiation [temple] by his blood, to be received by faith. (Rom. 3:23–25)

Revelation 12:10–11

In one short passage in the book of Revelation, John combines legal, military, and cultic metaphors to describe how Satan has been defeated by the blood of Christ and how God's people share in that victory:

> And I heard a loud voice in heaven, saying, "Now the salvation and the power and the kingdom of our God and the authority of his Christ have come, for the accuser [legal] of our brothers has been thrown down, who accuses them day and night before our God. And they have conquered [military] him by the blood of the Lamb [cultic] and by the word of their testimony, for they loved not their lives even unto death." (Rev. 12:10–11)

Hebrews 2:14–18

The author of Hebrews brings together various dimensions that have often been held apart in atonement theology:

> Since therefore the children share in flesh and blood, he himself likewise partook of the same things, that through death he might <u>destroy</u> [victory] the one who has the power of death, that is, the devil, and <u>deliver</u> [redemption] all those who through fear of death were subject to lifelong slavery. For surely it is not angels that he helps, but he helps the offspring of Abraham. Therefore he had to be made like his brothers in every respect, so that he might become a merciful and faithful high priest in the service of God, to make <u>propitiation</u> [sacrifice] for the sins of the people. For because he himself has suffered when tempted, he is <u>able to help</u> [example] those who are being tempted. (Heb. 2:14–18)

Integration throughout Church History

Unfortunately, the history of the doctrine of atonement has often been revised to fit into the mold of exclusive atonement theories. A typical survey covers the early church's "ransom theory," Anselm's "satisfaction theory," Abelard's "exemplarist theory," and Calvin's "penal substitution theory." These historical theories, as they are often taught, are assumed to be one-dimensional, mutually exclusive accounts of Christ's work on the cross. The problem with this approach is that while theologians have certainly focused on particular aspects of the atonement, most of them have done so within a broader framework that deeply appreciates the multidimensional work of Christ. A few representative examples will demonstrate that historically the church has not reduced Christ's atoning work to one aspect but rather has celebrated the fullness and integration of his multidimensional accomplishment on the cross.

While Anselm is often pigeonholed into a narrowly juridical approach to the atonement, he defies such neat categorization. In *Curs Deus Homo*, before even mentioning satisfaction, Anselm refers to the cross as Jesus's demonstration of love, recapitulation, and victory over evil.

> He <u>freed us</u> from our sins, and from his own <u>wrath</u>, and from hell, and from the power of the <u>devil</u>, whom he came to vanquish for us, because we were unable to do it, and purchased for us the kingdom of heaven; and by doing all these things, he <u>manifested the greatness of his love</u> toward us.[10]

Peter Abelard, while usually reduced to being an exemplarist, at least attempted to integrate the other dimensions:

> We have been <u>justified</u> by the blood of Christ and <u>reconciled</u> to God in this way: through this unique act of grace manifested to us—in that his Son has taken upon himself our nature and preserved therein in teaching us by word and <u>example</u> even unto death.[11]

John Calvin emphasized Christ bearing humanity's penalty, but he did so within a broader and integrated framework. The following is a snapshot:

> Clothed with our flesh he vanquished death and sin together that the <u>victory and triumph</u> might be ours. He offered as a <u>sacrifice</u> the flesh he received from us, that he

---

10. Anselm, "Why God Became Man," trans. Janet Fairweather, in *Anselm of Canterbury: The Major Works*, ed. Brian Davies and G. R. Evans, Oxford World's Classics (Oxford: Oxford University Press, 2008), 1.5.

11. Peter Abelard, "Exposition of the Epistle to the Romans (An Excerpt From the Second Book)," in *A Scholastic Miscellany: Anselm to Ockham*, ed. and trans. Eugene Fairweather, The Library of Christian Classics (Philadelphia: Westminster, 1956), 283.

might wipe out our guilt by his act of <u>expiation</u> and <u>appease the Father's righteous wrath</u>.[12]

The church has historically (at least up until the Enlightenment) embraced the multidimensional nature of the atonement and sought to integrate the dimensions as much as possible.

Integration in the Doctrine of Atonement

Having seen integration in Scripture and church history, we must now seek further synthesis in the doctrine of atonement today. As examples, I will integrate four sets of dimensions of Christ's atoning work.

Victory and Forgiveness

Scripture affirms the following two truths:

- Christ came to conquer the devil (1 John 3:8).
- Christ came to forgive sins (Mark 2:10).

Unfortunately, many Christians feel the need to choose one or the other, as if Christ came *either* to vanquish Satan *or* to forgive sin. Perhaps this is because whole theories have been built around these two dimensions—*Christus Victor* and penal substitution—and are often presented as mutually exclusive. Thankfully, many today recognize the need for a less reductionistic approach to the atonement and have sought to uphold Christ's victory and forgiveness. However, holding two aspects of Christ's work in coexisting tension is not enough when integration is possible. It is not a matter of which dimension is more important but rather how they fit together in the greater story of the kingdom of God.

---

12. John Calvin, *Institutes of the Christian Religion*, ed. John T. McNeill, trans. Ford Lewis Battles, 2 vols., Library of Christian Classics (Louisville: Westminster John Knox, 2006), 1:466–67 (2.12.3).

Victory and forgiveness are remedies to different but related problems: humanity's bondage to the devil (Eph. 2:2) and humanity's hostility with God (Rom. 1:18–3:20). The key, however, is to recognize that these two problems relate to one another in a particular way. Bondage to Satan is a result of enmity with God. In other words, humans are in the kingdom of Satan *because* they have rejected the kingdom of God. Enmity with God, therefore, is the root problem, with bondage to Satan being derivative. Because of human sin against God, the enemy rightly accuses people of their sin, shame, and penalty of death.

The order of humanity's sinful condition is determinative for the order of its remedy. Jesus defeats the devil by forgiving the sins of God's people, thereby nullifying the enemy's power of accusation. By dealing with the root problem of sin, Christ defangs the devil and delivers his people from the kingdom of darkness. Paul says, "Having forgiven us all of our trespasses" and "canceling the record of debt that stood against us" through his death on the cross, "he disarmed the rulers and authorities and put them to open shame" (Col. 2:13–15). The key issue, then, is *how* Christ conquered Satan. He did not do so through sheer force or naked power. Nor did he deceive the devil. Jesus triumphed through sacrificial love in such a way that upheld and revealed God's justice, wisdom, and mercy. By dying in the place of sinners, Jesus cancelled the debt of sin, setting God's people free from the power of the enemy.[13]

Propitiation and Example

While we have already seen the integration and ordering of objective and subjective approaches to the atonement, we

---

13. For a deeper exploration of victory through forgiveness, see Jeremy Treat, *The Crucified King: Atonement and Kingdom in Biblical and Systematic Theology* (Grand Rapids, MI: Zondervan, 2014), 193–226.

will now focus more specifically on integrating the dimensions of propitiation and example. We begin with 1 John 4:10–12, where both dimensions are present: "In this is love, not that we have loved God but that he loved us and sent his Son to be the propitiation for our sins. Beloved, if God so loved us, we also ought to love one another. No one has ever seen God; if we love one another, God abides in us and his love is perfected in us."

The key here is not merely that both dimensions are present but rather how they relate. The declaration of Jesus as the "propitiation for our sins" is immediately followed by the exhortation that "if God so loved us, we also ought to love one another." This does not present two options of what Christ accomplished but rather two dimensions that are interlocked in a particular order. Christ died for our sins, averting wrath and expiating sin. Therefore, because of his finished work, we are capable of and called to love one another.

What we see in 1 John 4:10–12 is common throughout the New Testament. Many of Scripture's statements about Christ's objective accomplishment in substitutionary atonement are paired with the subjective emphasis of following Jesus's example (Mark 10:32–45; John 13:1–17; 1 Pet. 2:21–25). This pattern shapes the entire book of Leviticus, with the first half focusing on how atonement makes God's people holy and the second half about how to walk in holiness. As Martin Luther says, "When you have Christ as the foundation and chief blessing of your salvation, then the other part follows: that you take him as your example."[14]

---

14. Martin Luther, "A Brief Instruction on What to Look For and Expect in the Gospels," in *Martin Luther's Basic Theological Writings*, ed. Timothy F. Lull and William R. Russel, 2nd ed. (Minneapolis: Fortress, 2005), 96.

Guilt and Shame

Guilt and shame are part of the human predicament. While some cultures are more shame-based and others more guilt-based, all cultures include both shame and guilt. It will not do to merely understand guilt for Western cultures and shame for Eastern cultures. Rather, we must uphold guilt and shame as part of the universal human problem and integrate them in Christ's atoning work.

Throughout the Old Testament, the concept of covenant integrates shame and guilt. When a covenant was broken, there were legal sanctions (guilt) and public ramifications (shame). In the New Testament, Romans 1–3 is a clear example of the integration of guilt and shame. While Romans 1 emphasizes God's wrath against unrighteousness (Rom. 1:18), it also frames sin in terms of honor and shame: "For although they knew God, they did not honor him as God" (Rom. 1:21). Sin, therefore, dishonors God, resulting in shame and guilt for the sinner.

In Romans 2, the law comes into play, but in conjunction with the honor-shame theme. Paul says, "You who boast in the law dishonor God by breaking the law" (Rom. 2:23). For the apostle Paul, guilt and shame are clearly interwoven in the sinful condition of humanity.

Jackson Wu says humanity has both an "honor-debt" (we have fallen short of God's glory and owe him the honor he deserves), and a "sin-debt" (we are guilty before God and need our debt to be forgiven).[15] Jesus deals with both debts by dying in our place. He bears our shame, restoring God's honor. He bears our guilt, forgiving our sins. This approach does not make either guilt or shame a means to the other, but it shows how closely they are related in terms of sin and atonement.

---

15. Jackson Wu, "How Christ Saves God's Face . . . and Ours: A Soteriology of Honor and Shame," *Missiology: An International Review* 44, no. 4 (2016): 379–80.

Adoption and Theosis

Adoption is one of the greatest blessings of Christ's atoning work on the cross. A biblical understanding of adoption, however, presses beyond its earthly limitations to a divine reality. Through the cross we share in the sonship of Christ. Therefore, when we are adopted in Christ, we become not merely a member of a family but also a participant in the triune life. Jesus prays to the Father about making his name known to his disciples, "that the love with which you have loved me may be in them, and I in them" (John 17:26). Therefore, the Father does not love us with a different love than that with which he loves the Son. Rather, we share in the Father's love for the Son. We participate in an infinitely loving relationship.

The overlap of adoption and theosis is also evident in Galatians 4:5, where Paul says that Christ came to bring redemption "so that we might receive adoption as sons." He then goes on to describe this adoption as being thoroughly Trinitarian: "And because you are sons, God has sent the Spirit of his Son into our hearts, crying, 'Abba! Father!'" (Gal. 4:6). The Spirit of the Son is in us crying out "Father" in such a way that draws us into the triune life as sons and daughters of God.

Integration of God's Attributes: Simply God

To have an integrated doctrine of atonement one must have an integrated view of God. As Moses declared, "The LORD is one" (Deut 6:4). In other words, God's love is not in competition with his wrath, nor is his mercy at odds with his justice. He does not whimsically move from anger to love or from delight to vengeance. The Lord always acts in line with his entire character and whole being. In everything he does, God is loving, just, wise, holy, and good—infinitely so. The church has traditionally affirmed this idea in what has been called the doctrine of divine simplicity.

Simplicity means that God is not made up of composite parts (wisdom, love, righteousness, and so on) but rather is one perfect essence through and through. God is not sometimes righteous and other times forgiving. He is not kind here and severe there. "I AM WHO I AM," declares God in divine self-revelation (Ex. 3:14). As Barth says, "His being is whole and undivided."[16] In other words, God is simply God. And our understanding of his attributes are human attempts to comprehend what our minds cannot fully behold—the divine essence. We can certainly speak of God's attributes, but in doing so we must recognize that they are distinct but without division. God is all of himself in all of his works.[17]

The difficulty that the doctrine of simplicity addresses (the seeming tension between attributes) is not with God's divine essence but with humanity's fallen understanding. We struggle to know how love and wrath can fit together, for example, because we have never experienced anger that is perfectly righteous nor love that is purely unselfish. Herman Bavinck writes, "There is no such thing as a conflict between God's justice and his love. In our sinful state it may appear to us that way, but in God all attributes are one and fully consistent with one another."[18] When we seek a coherent account of the doctrine of atonement, we do not attempt to

---

16. Karl Barth, *The Doctrine of God*, vol. 2/1 of *Church Dogmatics*, ed. G. W. Bromiley and Thomas Torrance, trans. G. W. Bromiley (Edinburgh: T&T Clark, 1958), 660.

17. We can also refer to God's attributes as his perfections, for in every attribute God is infinitely perfect. God is not merely holy. He is holy, holy, holy. He is infinitely wise, unendingly loving, and eternally compassionate. His love has no end. His grace never runs out. His kindness is without bounds. This means that there is no such thing as a universal, such as goodness, that exists outside of God that is then applied to him. God *is* good, and what we have come to know as goodness is an aspect of God's essence and character.

18. Herman Bavinck, *Sin and Salvation in Christ*, vol. 3 of *Reformed Dogmatics*, ed. John Bolt, trans. John Vriend (Grand Rapids, MI: Baker Academic, 2003), 369.

integrate God himself. We acknowledge the integrity of his being. The Lord is the one "with whom there is no variation" (James 1:17).[19]

This understanding of divine simplicity is helpful for maintaining an integrated, coherent doctrine of atonement. As revealed in the Old Testament, the fullness of God's character is involved in his dealing with sin. "The LORD, the LORD, a God merciful and gracious, slow to anger, and abounding in steadfast love and faithfulness, keeping steadfast love for thousands, forgiving iniquity and transgression and sin, but who will by no means clear the guilty" (Ex. 34:6–7). Yet what God revealed to Moses through words, he has revealed more vividly and fully through the incarnate Word—Jesus. For while different aspects of God's being and character are on display throughout Scripture, the cross is where we see that these attributes cohere as a whole. Through the cross, we see God's holiness and love, mercy and justice, majesty and meekness. As Kevin Vanhoozer says, "God is all that he is—all holy, all loving, all just—in all that he does. The cross, as the sum of divine wisdom, displays all the divine perfections."[20]

Having laid the foundation of divine simplicity, I will now show how several paradoxical sets of attributes or actions come together in perfect harmony in the cross.

---

19. It is important to acknowledge that we speak of the attributes of God in a different way than we speak of the attributes of people. The attributes of God are essential to his being: God *is* just. God *is* wise. And so on. Whereas for creation, it is almost never that way. I might say that Stephen Curry *is* athletic, but that is not essential to his being. If Stephen Curry loses his athleticism, he does not cease to be Stephen Curry. Or again, I might say that Los Angeles *is* a large city. But when Los Angeles was a small pueblo of forty-four people in 1781, it was still Los Angeles. The claim that "God is holy," however, does not depend on a season or situation. God *is* holy in a way that is essential to his being and will always be true in the fullest sense.

20. Kevin Vanhoozer, "Atonement," in *Mapping Modern Theology: A Thematic and Historical Introduction*, ed. Kelly Kapic and Bruce McCormack (Grand Rapids, MI: Baker Academic, 2012), 201.

Wrath and Love

The love of God and the wrath of God are commonly pitted against one another, particularly in the doctrine of atonement. If the cross is the demonstration of the love of God, then how could it also be an expression of his wrath?

This dichotomy arises from a sentimentalized view of love and a caricature of wrath. In our society, love is often reduced to affection or affirmation. To love someone is either to have warm feelings toward them or to affirm them without conditions. And when people in our society think of the wrath of God, they imagine a red-faced deity with a bad temper and short fuse. This irritable God lashes out with uncontrollable rage and finds pleasure in punishing the wicked. These understandings of God's love and wrath are grossly unwarranted.

We know from our own experience that anger and love can coexist. I love my children deeply. And when their disobedience leads to harm, I have an appropriate anger that does not drive out my love but comes alongside it. Furthermore, to say that love and anger can coexist does not actually go far enough. Anger arises *because* of love. Because I love my children, I would rightfully be angry if anyone attempted to hurt them. If I did not have anger in this situation, one would be right to question whether I do, in fact, love my children. Anger rises and falls with love.

When we apply this to God, we begin to see how his love and wrath cohere in his perfect character. God's love is not blind affirmation but a holy love that confronts evil from a place of care. God's wrath is not a shaken can of irritability waiting to explode on otherwise innocent and unknowing people. God does respond to sin and evil with a righteous anger, but he is slow to anger and always acts in accordance with his perfect character. The wrath of God is not incompatible with the love of God but rather arises for the purpose of protecting what he loves.

We must understand that wrath is not an attribute of God. God is love. God is holy. God is just. God is not wrath. God's wrath is the rightful expression of his holy love in the face of sin and evil. Before the foundations of the earth, the triune God had perfect love, joy, holiness, and peace. There was no wrath because there was no sin. God's wrath arises from his holy love in opposition to wickedness. Wrath only exists where sin exists. Therefore, we should uphold the priority of God's love and the necessity of God's wrath to safeguard his love in a fallen world.

To speak of the wrath of God, however, moves beyond the emotion of anger to the action of righteous judgment. How can God judge and condemn people he loves? At the most basic level, to hold evil accountable is loving. To defend and protect people from injustice is loving. Yet the greatest display of judgment flowing from love is the cross of Christ. At the cross, the wrath of God was poured out on the sin of the world (Rom. 3:25)—driven by the love of God (John 3:16). Through the wisdom of the cross, the love of God satisfies the wrath of God to redeem the people of God. This is God simply being God. It may appear to us that the cross resolves tension in the different aspects of God's character. But God is who he is in all that he does. The cross does not resolve God's character but rather reveals his character. The Lord confronts wickedness and evil with wrath, not in spite of love but because of his love.

Mercy and Justice

Can God be both merciful and just? If God is merciful by excusing sinners from punishment, is it not a miscarriage of justice? Would a judge be honorable if she let an offender go free? Does not God have to choose between mercy and justice?

The Old Testament makes especially clear that mercy and justice are not in opposition. Take, for example, this command:

> What does the LORD require of you?
> To act justly and to love mercy
>   and to walk humbly with your God. (Mic. 6:8 NIV)

The Hebrew word for "justice" (*mishpat*) means to treat people equitably regardless of their race, gender, sex, or class. It means giving people their due, whether punishment of wrongdoing or the protection of rights. Yet while we are called to administer justice, we must do so with a posture of mercy. The Hebrew word for "mercy" (*hesed*) refers to God's undeserved yet devoted love. Just as God has been merciful to us, we are called to be merciful to others. Furthermore, doing justice in the Old Testament often includes mercy, with particular concern for the most vulnerable of society, such as the poor, widows, orphans, and immigrants. Gleaning laws in the Old Testament are one example of how doing justice involves giving mercy (Lev. 19:9–10).[21]

Mercy and justice are not a zero-sum balance, such that to be merciful one must sacrifice justice or vice versa. One cannot be truly merciful without being just, and one cannot be truly just without being merciful. While the two are difficult to hold together in fallen humanity, God himself displays the perfect harmony of mercy and justice. God does not go back and forth between being merciful and just. He brings the fullness of himself in all of his work and is, therefore, merciful and just in all that he does. And while we see this throughout God's dealings with Israel, God's mercy and justice are most clearly on display in his Son.

Many people know that Jesus came to bring mercy, but fewer recognize that he also came to bring justice. In the book of Isaiah, the Lord expresses the Messiah's mission in this way:

---

21. This paragraph draws heavily from Timothy Keller, *Generous Justice: How God's Grace Makes Us Just* (New York: Penguin, 2010).

"I have put my Spirit upon him; he will bring forth justice to the nations" (Isa. 42:1). Jesus made his mission of mercy and justice clear when he opened up the scroll of Isaiah in the synagogue and declared,

> The Spirit of the Lord is upon me,
>> because he has anointed me
>> to proclaim good news to the poor.
> He has sent me to proclaim liberty to the captives
>> and recovering of sight to the blind,
>> to set at liberty those who are oppressed,
> to proclaim the year of the Lord's favor. (Luke 4:18–19)

Jesus is the embodiment of mercy and justice. And when he taught his disciples, he referred to mercy and justice as "the weightier matters of the law" (Matt. 23:23). But it was at the cross where mercy and justice were displayed in their most gloriously divine juxtaposition. The cross is the ultimate exhibit of God's judgment being poured out on sin. The cross is also the definitive showcase of God's mercy, for on it Christ bore the judgment of sinners so that they may be saved.

Power and Service

Power and service often seem opposites. In most cultures, the more powerful people are, the less likely they are to serve. Furthermore, the widespread abuse of power—whether by politicians or pastors—has led many to see power as inherently corrupt. How do power and service relate for God, and particularly in the atonement?

Jesus's most significant teaching on power took place not in the temple (the religious center), in the Sanhedrin (the political center), or in the city gates (the cultural center)—but instead on the road to the cross (Mark 10:32–45). When two of the disciples asked Jesus to sit at his right and left hand in his glory, Jesus did not rebuke their demand. He redirected their desire:

> You know that those who are considered rulers of the Gentiles lord it over them, and their great ones exercise authority over them. But it shall not be so among you. But whoever would be great among you must be your servant, and whoever would be first among you must be slave of all. (Mark 10:42–44)

Jesus is teaching that there are two kinds of power (or at least two uses of power). Let's call them "worldly power" and "kingdom power." Worldly power seeks to use whatever position or privilege one has for one's own benefit, even if it comes at the expense of others. Jesus says, "It shall not be so among you." There is a different kind of power.

> Worldly power is used for selfish ambition.
> Kingdom power is used for sacrificial love.
>
> Worldly power exploits the weaknesses of others.
> Kingdom power equips others in their strengths.
>
> Worldly power is self-seeking.
> Kingdom power is self-denying.
>
> Worldly power is used to suppress.
> Kingdom power is used to serve.
>
> Worldly power builds up self at the expense of others.
> Kingdom power lays one's life down for others.

After Jesus teaches about these two kinds of powers, he uses the opportunity to explain the meaning of his death: "For even the Son of Man came not to be served but to serve, and to give his life as a ransom for many" (Mark 10:45). Jesus had already told his disciples three times *that* he was going to die. But here he tells them *why* he is going to die. Jesus is the Messiah who came to bring the kingdom of God, but he does so as the suffering servant who dies in our place for our sins. Christ exercises power through service.

The Harmony of Atonement

The multidimensional work of Christ on the cross is like an orchestra playing a beautiful symphony. In an orchestra, each instrument and note uniquely matter, and they come together to create a musical composition that is greater than the mere combination of the parts. The atonement is a symphony "to the praise of his glorious grace" (Eph. 1:6), and it is essential that each dimension coheres together in unity. However, for the members of an orchestra to be in tune with one another, they traditionally begin a concert by tuning to one note (an "A") from one instrument (the oboe). In other words, by tuning to a common source, the various instruments create a beautiful harmony.

The same is true for the doctrine of atonement. While we must seek to integrate dimensions with one another, they ultimately find coherence in their common connection to Christ dying in our place for our sins. Christ crucified is our righteousness, our redemption, and our sanctification (1 Cor. 1:23, 30). "In him all things hold together" (Col. 1:17). Such a multidimensional and integrated doctrine of atonement is not only true but also beautiful.

5

The Community
of Atonement

Reconciled and Reconciling

*But now in Christ Jesus you who once were
far off have been brought near by the blood
of Christ. For he himself is our peace, who
has made us both one and has broken down
in his flesh the dividing wall of hostility.*
EPHESIANS 2:13–14

*Jesus Christ has a cure for the evils of racism, tribalism,
and divided humanity. . . . In Christ, both Jews and
Gentiles are one. They have become a new community,
the church. What made this possible was the atoning
work of Christ on the cross, which destroyed their
enmity and brought reconciliation and peace.*[1]
YUSUFU TURAKI

---

1. Yusufu Turaki, "Ephesians," in *Africa Bible Commentary: A One-Volume Commentary Written by 70 African Scholars*, ed. Tokunboh Adeyemo (Nairobi, Kenya: WordAlive, 2006), 1456.

Vivek Murthy was the surgeon general of the United States and encountered a variety of medical problems throughout his career. And yet, reflecting on his time as a doctor, Murthy made a shocking claim: "During my years caring for patients, the most common pathology I saw was not heart disease or diabetes, it was loneliness."[2] Murthy goes on to say that our society today is experiencing a "loneliness epidemic," which most people can identify with based not on years of research but on their own lived experience. Furthermore, our attempts to satisfy our longing for relational intimacy with social media have led not to deep relational intimacy but rather to shallow digital connectedness. Can the cross of Christ speak to the loneliness and isolation in our lives?

The problem of personal loneliness is also coupled with increasing societal fragmentation. Political lines have divided families, churches, and our nation. Racial injustice has created tension across ethnic lines throughout the world. International warfare has brought about fear of nuclear threat and the undoing of the global economy. Can the cross of Christ speak to the fragmentation in our society today?

Unfortunately, for many Christians the cross has little to say to our personal lonesomeness or social ills. Too many churches have reduced the death of Christ to a message of individual salvation that affects the eternity of our souls while having little significance for our communities today. But a narrow view of the cross leads to a truncated view of Christianity. Such an approach to the Christian life amounts to self-centered spirituality based on personal preference, where the church exists as a dispenser of spiritual goods to prop up my individual

---

2. Vivek Murthy, "Work and the Loneliness Epidemic," *Harvard Business Review*, September 26, 2017, https://hbr.org/.

relationship with God. Of course, community still has a role to play in this approach to the faith, but it is merely another consumer good that I use on my journey of self-discovery and self-improvement.

The Christian answer to the relational and societal brokenness of the world is the cross of Christ. Therefore, we must recover the communal nature of Christ's atoning death so that we can experience cross-shaped community and speak prophetically to our divided world. We must not reduce community to a mere implication of the atonement. The atonement is intrinsically communal.

In this chapter, we will first explore how the cross creates community. We must not separate the vertical dimension of Christ's death from its horizontal implications, and we must not overlook the fact that Christ's reconciled people have a ministry and message of reconciliation. The atoning work of Christ creates a new community—the church—that is called to witness to Christ's kingdom throughout the world. Second, we will consider the identity of this cross-shaped community. The atoning death of Christ makes a sacramental, political, just, multiethnic, and unified community.

The Cross and Community

The death of Jesus is a community-creating event, at once saving us from our sins and making us a people bound together by love. Community, therefore, is not on the periphery of the doctrine of atonement but at its core. Jesus died to adopt orphans into a family, to gather his wayward sheep into a flock, and to transfer citizens into a new kingdom. To understand the communal nature of the atonement, we must begin by talking about the vertical and horizontal dimensions of Christ's work.

Vertical and Horizontal

Ephesians 2:1–10 emphasizes the vertical dimensions of salvation—namely, how those who were dead in sin have been raised to life and seated in the heavenly realm with Christ. Through the gospel, we have been reconciled with God. Ephesians 2:11–22 then talks about the horizontal aspects of salvation. While the "dividing wall of hostility" was a barrier between Jews and Gentiles (Eph. 2:14), Christ dealt with ethnic division at its root and thereby demolished the dividing wall, bringing Jews and Gentiles together as one people. Through his death, Christ put to death the hostility between people and replaced it with peace. He took our sinful animosity to the grave with him and left it there when he rose.

The death of the Messiah reconciles sinners to God and to one another—and you cannot have one without the other. This is why Scripture most commonly speaks of Christ dying "for *us*" (Rom. 5:8) or "for *our* sins" (1 Cor. 15:3), although there are times to acknowledge that Christ "gave himself for *me*" (Gal. 2:20). Whereas Western Christians tend to think of the individual as the basic element of Christianity and community as an implication or complement, Scripture puts the community at the core, with the individual finding his or her place within this relational matrix. Again, community is not an implication of atonement but rather is intrinsic to atonement. The blood of Christ creates a new covenant community, where God's declaration over us is "I will be your God, and you will be my people."

The shape of the cross itself is a constant reminder of the comprehensive nature of Christ's work: the vertical beam of the cross is a symbol of the reconciliation between God and sinners, while the horizontal beam is a symbol of God reconciling sinners to one another. As Sung Wook Chung says, "Salvation has to do not only with vertical reconciliation between God and humanity but also with horizontal reconciliation between human beings."[3]

Reconciled and Reconciling

The reconciling work of God in Christ not only comes *to* us but also flows *through* us to those around us. The blessed become a blessing to others. The justified become doers of justice. The recipients of peace become peacemakers. And as we learn in 2 Corinthians 5, the reconciled become ambassadors of reconciliation:

> All this is from God, who through Christ reconciled us to himself and gave us the ministry of reconciliation; that is, in Christ God was reconciling the world to himself, not counting their trespasses against them, and entrusting to us the message of reconciliation. Therefore, we are ambassadors for Christ, God making his appeal through us. We implore you on behalf of Christ, be reconciled to God. (2 Cor. 5:18–20)

The message of reconciliation refers to the proclamation of the good news of Jesus—the announcement that by grace through faith people can be reconciled to God and not have their trespasses counted against them because Christ has borne those trespasses on the cross. But the message of reconciliation comes within a broader ministry of reconciliation. In Christ, God was reconciling *the world* to himself. Followers of Jesus, therefore, are called to live in light of the new reality created by Christ—namely, that he has accomplished all that is necessary

---

3. Sung Wook Chung, "Salvation as Reconciliation: Toward a Theology of Reconciliation in the Division of the Korean Peninsula," in *So Great a Salvation: Soteriology in the Majority World*, ed. Gene L. Green, Stephen T. Pardue, and K. K. Yeo (Grand Rapids, MI: Eerdmans, 2017), 140.

for vertical and horizontal reconciliation. We are sent out as witnesses to the reconciling power of Christ's death and its availability through faith in the crucified one.

Our ongoing work of reconciliation must be grounded in Christ's finished work on the cross. As Dietrich Bonhoeffer says, "Christian brotherhood is not an ideal which we must realize; it is rather a reality created by God in Christ in which we may participate."[4] The church does not accomplish reconciliation. It receives and reflects the reconciliation already accomplished by Christ. Paul does not tell the church to *attain* but rather "to *maintain* the unity of the Spirit" (Eph. 4:3). All our work is grounded in Christ's objective work.

Atonement and the Church

The atoning work of Christ must be understood within the unfolding theme in Scripture of God forming a people for himself. Throughout the Old Testament, the Lord called and fashioned his people Israel through suffering in Egypt, the fulfillment of promises in Canaan, and exile in Babylon. But at the heart of this formation of his covenant people was the sacrificial system, housed in the tabernacle and then the temple. The book of Leviticus makes clear that atonement for sin is a crucial part of the holy God's plan to form a holy people.

Israel's purpose, however, was not merely to be a holy nation but to be a vehicle for God to create a people of many nations (Isa. 2:1–5; 49:6). And it was ultimately through Israel's Messiah that Jews and Gentiles would come together as one people in the church. Jesus said, "I will build my church" (Matt. 16:18), and when he went to the cross, that is exactly what he did. The cross creates a community of sinners saved by grace. But it is not a generic community. Through the blood of Christ,

---

4. Dietrich Bonhoeffer, *Life Together* (San Francisco: HarperSanFrancisco, 1993), 30.

we are saved into the church. As Paul says, "Christ loved the church and gave himself up for her" (Eph. 5:25).

The cross, however, not only creates the church but also shapes its very existence. The crucified Messiah forges a cruciform people. In other words, the atonement is the power and the pattern for community in the church:

- We love one another as Christ has loved us (John 13:35).
- We forgive one another as Christ has forgiven us (Eph. 4:32).
- We serve one another as Christ has served us (Mark 10:32–45).

The grace of God makes the church not just a better version of the world's community but a different kind of community altogether. The church is the community of the gospel, a place for sinners and sufferers who acknowledge their need for Jesus and each other.

I will never forget when my wife and I visited Israel and went to the Church of the Nativity in Bethlehem. To enter the church building, one must walk through "The Humbling Door," which is appropriately titled because the door is under five feet tall, requiring a person to bow down to fit under the door frame. As we entered humbly, we also realized that we were entering vulnerably, coming into a room in a defenseless position. The cross is the great humbling door of the church. We enter with humility and vulnerability, knowing that we have come not based on our own merits but through God's undeserving grace. The cross is not only the entrance into the church but also creates a culture of humility and vulnerability in the church. As John Stott says, "The community of Christ is the community of the cross. Having been brought into being by the cross, it continues to live by and under the cross."[5]

---

5. John Stott, *The Cross of Christ* (Downers Grove, IL: InterVarsity Press, 1986), 256.

While the atonement creates the church, it does so within a greater vision for the eternal kingdom of God. Christ is the King who "has freed us from our sins by his blood and made us a kingdom" (Rev. 1:5–6). Therefore, the church is the community of the cross-shaped kingdom amid a world still in rebellion against the King. One day the church will give way to the kingdom. But today, in between the already and the not yet of the kingdom, the local church is the heart of God's work in the world as a sign and foretaste of the kingdom. God advances his kingdom through the church as it conforms to the cross. Indeed, the kingdom has come, but in this age it is hidden beneath the folly of the cross (1 Cor. 1:18).

The Atonement Creates a Particular Community

As we have seen, the atonement is a community-creating event and, more specifically, is the foundation of and formative power for the church. We will now focus on five aspects of the church's identity that are shaped by its source in the atonement.

The Atonement Creates a Sacramental Community

One of the ways that the church is anchored to Christ's atoning work is through the sacraments, particularly baptism and the Lord's Supper. Baptism represents initial entry into God's family, while communion signifies ongoing nourishment within God's family. Both are rooted in Christ's atoning work and keep the church tethered to that which birthed it in the first place.

Baptism is a picture of God's grace and a profession of our faith. When a person is plunged into the waters of baptism, it is a visible expression of dying to the old self and being buried with Christ. Arising from the water is a representation of rising with Christ from the dead, transformed for new life. As

Paul says in Romans 6:4, "We were buried therefore with him by baptism into death, in order that, just as Christ was raised from the dead by the glory of the Father, we too might walk in newness of life." While baptism represents the entry point into the church for a new believer, it also provides an opportunity for all believers to remember their own baptism and the reality to which it points. We are daily called to die to our flesh and live in Christ. Baptism is a symbol of believers' union with their crucified and resurrected Savior.

The Lord's Supper is a sign of God's provision for the ongoing nourishment of his redeemed people through the body and blood of Jesus. Just as Israel was given manna in the wilderness, Christ's flesh and blood sustain God's people so that they can endure faithfully while living in the tension between the already and not yet of the kingdom of God. Furthermore, the bread and the cup remind the church of the costly grace that we receive in Christ. Christ's body was broken so that we could be made whole. His blood was shed so that we could be washed clean. Jesus is "our Passover lamb" (1 Cor. 5:7), and his blood is the "blood of the covenant" (Matt. 26:28). The Lord's Supper is a family meal, and we are God's children who have been given a place at the table. And while the emblems of the bread and cup are often small, they are a foretaste of the wedding supper of the Lamb. We remember the Lord's death during Communion, but it is also an act of hope looking into the future. "For as often as you eat this bread and drink the cup, you proclaim the Lord's death until he comes" (1 Cor. 11:26).

Each Sunday, the church gathers to retell the story of the gospel and recenter our lives around the God of the gospel. The sacraments are at the heart of this, tangibly reminding the church of Christ's atoning work and our participation in his cruciform love. In an increasingly digital and disembodied age, the sacraments are a profound way to cultivate our hearts toward following our crucified Messiah together as an embodied community.

The Atonement Creates a Political Community

The crucifixion of Christ was a political event. The process was overseen by a political ruler and carried out by Roman centurions, all of whom wielded the authority of the empire. Jesus was crucified as the "King of the Jews," an overtly political title. And his disciples declared "Jesus is Lord" in a context where "Caesar is Lord" was the common expression of allegiance. Even the Jews who cried out for his crucifixion had political motivations. Many were expecting a conquering Messiah who would overthrow Rome and establish a political kingdom. Yet, while those responsible for Christ's death were driven by political ends, Christ himself had an even greater political aim, although one that was different from and subversive to the politics of the world. Through his death on the cross, Jesus was establishing the kingdom of God. He who hung on the cross held the government of the world on his shoulders. Christ is a King who reigns with sacrificial love.

The politics of Jesus must be clearly distinguished from the political landscape in America, lest one be tempted to merely place Jesus on one side of the political aisle. Jesus is political but not partisan. He is neither a Republican nor a Democrat. Jesus is King of kings and Lord of lords. Our goal, therefore, is not to locate Jesus on the political spectrum of left and right but to recognize that Jesus is creating a different kind of community altogether. The Son of God is not campaigning for a party; he is building a kingdom.

The atoning work of Christ, therefore, creates a political community. But, again, the church is political in a different kind of way. The politics of Christ's people finds its shape within the story of the kingdom that has the cross as its apex. The blood of Christ ransoms us into the kingdom of God, within which we are restored to our creation purpose of ruling on God's behalf (Gen. 1:28). The church is a royal priesthood, representing God's loving reign on earth as it is in heaven (1 Pet. 2:9).

This means that while Christians are earthly citizens who have an obligation to our local and national governments (Rom. 13:1–7), we ultimately submit to the kingship of Christ. We are dual citizens, but loyalty to the city of God shapes and overrides allegiance to the earthly city. When Jesus says, "Render to Caesar the things that are Caesar's, and to God the things that are God's" (Mark 12:17), he is not minimizing the importance of politics but rather putting it in its place. In other words, Jesus is saying to give your taxes to the government but give your allegiance to God. The outcome is clear for God's people: kingdom over country.

The cruciform kingdom also reforms the way we think about political power. Christians must acknowledge the constant temptation to use political power to accomplish the church's purpose. And US history reveals that this allure applies to both sides of the political aisle. But the church is not a voting bloc or a campaign platform. The church is the household of God and an embassy of his kingdom. If the biblically rooted commitments of the church do not fit neatly into one side of the two-party system, then so be it. The church does not find its identity on the political spectrum but from the cross, which gives a new way of thinking about politics altogether.

The atonement creates a community that neither withdraws from politics nor becomes seduced by politics but instead engages politically in a way that is grounded in the cruciform kingdom of Christ. After all, nations rise and fall, and governments come and go, but the kingdom of Christ will stand forevermore.[6]

The Atonement Creates a Just Community

The atoning work of Christ creates a community that is devoted to mercy and justice. In other words, the cruciform ethics of Christ produce a counterintuitive ethic for the church:

- We pray for our enemies.
- We bless those who curse.
- We return love for hate.
- We use power to serve.

It is not as if there is one view of justice that everyone agrees on and simply needs to work toward. Rather, as Alasdair McIntyre has demonstrated, one's view of justice is shaped by his or her broader narrative of the world.[7] For Christians, therefore, our understanding of justice must be shaped by the story of the kingdom that culminates in the cross. The atoning work of Christ on the cross forms Christian ethics in at least three ways.

First, the cross levels the playing field and creates an understanding of mutual brokenness. Nobody holds their head high when standing at the foot of the cross. For there we learn how wretched is our transgression. We are all made in the image of God, yet we are all broken in our sin. The cross, therefore, sweeps the legs out from under condescension. The death of Christ enables us to embrace our mutual brokenness and our

---

6. Peter Leithart says, "We are social and political creatures. If humanity is going to achieve a state of health (what Christians call salvation), we are going to have to be saved in our social and political situations; our social structures and political institutions are going to have to become conducive to harmony and justice, peace and human flourishing." Peter Leithart, *Delivered from the Elements of the World: Atonement, Justification, and Mission* (Downers Grove, IL: IVP Academic, 2016), 13.

7. Alasdair MacIntyre, *Whose Justice? Which Rationality?* (Notre Dame, IN: University of Notre Dame Press, 1988).

mutual need for the grace of God in Christ. As Miroslav Volf says, "No one can be in the presence of the God of the crucified Messiah for long . . . without transposing the enemy from the sphere of monstrous humanity into the sphere of shared humanity and herself from the sphere of proud innocence into the sphere of common sinfulness."[8] There is no way to look down on others when on your knees at the cross.

Second, the cross breaks the cycle of injustice. Martin Luther King Jr. recognized the way that violence begets violence and hate begets hate, creating a cycle of injustice and resulting in what he called the "chain reaction of evil."[9] One of the ways that injustice compounds is through attempted solutions that do not address injustice itself but merely seek to replace the oppressor with the oppressed. Richard Bauckham discusses the pattern of the oppressed taking the place of the oppressor and writes, "The cross is the event in which the cycle is definitively broken."[10] Jesus breaks the cycle of injustice by responding to the greatest injustice of the world with love. He defeats hate through mercy. Christ dies, not to reverse the positions of the oppressed and the oppressor but rather to redeem both and make them family by grace.

Third, the cross motivates God's people toward mercy and justice. While believers can certainly partner with unbelievers in the work of justice, we do so with a distinctly Christian motivation. We are driven not by a secular vision of realizing human potential but by the conviction that every person is made in the image of God. We are motivated not by hate or vengeance but rather by gratitude and love, grounded in the gospel of Jesus

---

8. Miroslav Volf, *Exclusion and Embrace: A Theological Exploration of Identity, Otherness, and Reconciliation* (Nashville: Abingdon, 1996), 124.

9. Martin Luther King Jr., *Strength to Love* (Minneapolis: Fortress, 2010), 47.

10. Richard Bauckham, "Reading Scripture as a Coherent Story," in *The Art of Reading Scripture*, ed. Ellen Davis and Richard Hays (Grand Rapids, MI: Eerdmans, 2003), 52.

Christ. As people who have been justified by grace through faith, we seek justice for all. Scripture is clear that a true grasp of the gospel leads to reflecting God's heart for the poor and marginalized.

Through Christ's atoning work on the cross, God gives us a new heart, one that reflects his compassion for the most vulnerable people in society. The gospel makes us a people of mercy and justice.

The Atonement Creates a Multiethnic Community

When Jesus died on the cross, the sign above him read "King of the Jews" in three different languages (John 19:19–20). Pointing to a truth far beyond the intention of the Romans, the sign was right: the crucified one truly is a King who was building a kingdom of every tribe, language, people, and nation.

God's plan has always been to make a multiethnic, multinational, multicultural people, united in his Son by the Spirit. God promised Abram that his lineage would be a blessing to all families of the earth (Gen. 12:1–3). God called Israel to be his instrument for blessing the nations (Isa. 49:6). Although God's people failed to fulfill their calling, Jesus came as a descendent of Abraham and the true embodiment of Israel to fulfill God's promise. And while Jesus fulfilled Israel's calling with this life, he bore the curse of their sin through his death. "Christ redeemed us from the curse of the law by becoming a curse for us" (Gal. 3:13). Theologians often appeal to this verse for substitutionary atonement (rightly so), but it is commonly separated from its broader context of God fulfilling his promise to Abraham. The next verse declares that Jesus took our place on the cross "so that in Christ Jesus the blessing of Abraham might come to the Gentiles" (Gal. 3:14). Christ's atoning work not only reconciles sinners to God but also gathers the nations into one family, bound in a covenant through the blood of Christ.

Christ's atonement is not only for the salvation of different ethnic groups but also for the unification of those people into one kingdom. It is not enough for Jesus to make atonement for different ethnic groups while they remain separated by cultural differences. Christ died to tear down "the dividing wall of hostility" between Jews and Gentiles "that he might create in himself one new man in place of the two, so making peace, and might reconcile us both to God in one body through the cross, thereby killing the hostility" (Eph. 2:14–16). There will be no segregation in the new creation. Rather, the cross creates a multicultural kingdom of people who embrace their differences and unite in their Savior. As Athanasius says, "It is only on the cross that a man dies with arms outstretched . . . that He might draw His ancient people with the one and the Gentiles with the other, and join both together in himself."[11]

The disciple John stood at the foot of the cross when Jesus died outside Jerusalem. But as an old man later in life, he had another vision of how the Messiah's death would reach the ends of the earth:

> I looked, and behold, a great multitude that no one could number, from every nation, from all tribes and peoples and languages, standing before the throne and before the Lamb, clothed in white robes, with palm branches in their hands, and crying out with a loud voice, "Salvation belongs to our God who sits on the throne, and to the Lamb!" (Rev. 7:9–10)

---

11. Athanasius, *On the Incarnation*, trans. and ed. a Religious of C.S.M.V. (Crestwood, NY: St. Vladimir's Seminary Press, 2002), 55 (4.25).

The heavenly scene stretches the imagination. Myriads of people from every nation have come together to worship Christ the King. The voices resound in countless languages, dialects, and accents, coming from people with different color skin, facial features, and texture of hair—all equally yet uniquely imaging God. And, of course, the diversity goes beyond physical appearance. These "nations" are *ethnoi*, people groups who bring to the throne of the crucified one their cultural differences. Yet, amid the diversity, there is harmony and singlemindedness because it is all directed in worship to the Jewish Messiah, the one who died to ransom sinners into a multicultural kingdom.[12]

My church in Los Angeles has people from over one hundred and fifteen different nations. The cultural differences that we have certainly create tension at times. Yet we believe that the cross has made us one family from many nations. And as we learn to embrace our cultural differences, they deepen the unity that we have in Christ. As a community that comes together at the foot of the cross, we have an opportunity to show the reconciling power of the gospel to a world divided by sin.

The Atonement Creates a United Community

Our society has been marred by political fragmentation, racial tension, and deep-seated division. Even worse, the division in the world has crept into the church. The body of Christ today is divided over politics, race, and secondary doctrines. Yet Jesus died for the unity of the church—one of the glorious achievements of the atonement. Through the cross, he has made us one (Eph. 2:14–15).

---

12. I believe that the rising recognition of global theology in the West presents an unprecedented opportunity to discover new and richer perspectives on Christ's atoning work. For an introduction to numerous majority-world theologians, see Gene L. Green, Stephen T. Pardue, and K. K. Yeo, eds., *Majority World Theology: Christian Doctrine in Global Context* (Grand Rapids, MI: Eerdmans, 2020).

Paul discusses the unity of the church at length in 1 Corinthians. The young church had divided into factions, and many were associating with their preferred leaders: "I follow Paul," or "I follow Apollos," or "I follow Cephas" (1 Cor. 1:12). Paul asks, "Is Christ divided? Was Paul crucified for you?" (1 Cor. 1:13), implying that the crucifixion of Jesus purchased a unity for them that they were attempting to undo with their splintering. How, then, does Paul lead this divided church toward unity? He appeals to his foundational message: "Christ crucified" (1 Cor. 1:23). The cross is the basis for the unity of the church.

The practical nature of the book of 1 Corinthians reveals the real-life unity that the Lord desires for his church. We often assume that messiness and conflict are barriers to unity. Xiaxia Xue, a New Testament scholar from Hong Kong, talks about how we assume unity is a peaceful state with a lack of conflict or tension. In other words, we see conflict as an outlier, something that intrudes from time to time to threaten our unity. She concludes, however, "The essence of the church is the community in union with Christ *in the midst of conflict.*"[13] Unity is not the absence of conflict. It is the result of dealing with conflict in a healthy way. This vision of community is rooted in Christ's atoning death. His body was broken to make us whole. The cross is the way into the community of Christ and shapes the way we function as the community of Christ. We die daily to self and live for Christ, his people, and his mission.

For followers of Jesus, what we have in common in Christ is greater than any differences we have outside of him. Because of God's grace, our unity in Jesus is greater than our differences

13. Xiaxia E. Xue, "The Community as Union with Christ in the Midst of Conflict: An Ecclesiology of the Pauline Letters from a Chinese Perspective," in *The Church from Every Tribe and Tongue: Ecclesiology in the Majority World*, ed. Gene L. Green, Stephen T. Pardue, and K. K. Yeo (Grand Rapids, MI: Eerdmans, 2018), 114 (emphasis added).

in politics, race, cultural background, or socioeconomic status. In 1 Corinthians 1:9, Paul reminds the church, "You were called into the fellowship of his Son, Jesus Christ." The Greek word for "fellowship" is *koinōnia*, which refers to community relationships brought about through *common* participation in something.[14] Fellowship happens when a group of people have something in common, whether a hobby, sports team, or political party. That commonality is what brings them together and makes them a community. For Christians, what we have in common is Christ. We are one people because we are united in our one Savior.

Conclusion

As the Messiah suffered on the cross, abandoned by most of his disciples, below him stood his mother, Mary, and his beloved friend, John. From the cross, Jesus declared to his mother, "Woman, behold, your son!" and then said to John, "Behold, your mother!" (John 19:26–27). Mary and John were able to experience in that moment what would be true of God's people for all time: we have been adopted in the family of God by the blood of Jesus (Eph. 1:5–7). Through Christ's atoning death, we are sons and daughters, brothers and sisters, fathers and mothers (1 Tim. 5:1).

Our reconciliation to God and to one another are inseparable. Think of it like this: I am the second of four children. So when I was born into the world, I was born simultaneously as a son and a brother. It is not that I am in essence a son and then by function a brother. They are inseparable. So it is with the church. Jesus is our older brother (Heb. 2:11–12), and when we are adopted into the family of God through the

---

14. See J. Hainz, "κοινωνία," in *Exegetical Dictionary of the Greek New Testament*, 3 vols. (Grand Rapids, MI: Eerdmans, 1991), 2:303–5.

blood of Christ, we are simultaneously God's children and one another's siblings.

In this chapter, I have tried to explode the notion that Jesus died so that I could have "my personal relationship with God." Of course, God loves us as individuals, but not in an individualistic way. The death of the Messiah is for the forgiveness of sins but also for the formation of a community and the renewal of the world. The church is not an afterthought to salvation. The church is not an extracurricular activity to following Jesus. The church is not an optional add-on for spirituality. The church is the community of the gospel and is at the heart of why Jesus went to the cross in the first place.

6

The Life of Atonement

Taking Up Your Cross

*If anyone would come after me, let him deny himself
and take up his cross daily and follow me.*
LUKE 9:23

*Jesus laid down the requirements for those who
wanted to be members of the kingdom as true
followers of the Messiah. . . . Take up one's cross.*[1]
VICTOR BABAJIDE COLE

The doctrine of atonement unfortunately does not influence
the day-to-day lives of many Christians. Perhaps this is because theology in general is often perceived as an academic
discipline removed from life in the "real world." Maybe it

---

1. Victor Babajide Cole, "Mark," in *Africa Bible Commentary: A One-Volume Commentary Written by 70 African Scholars*, ed. Tokunboh Adeyemo (Nairobi, Kenya:
WordAlive, 2006), 1211.

is because people reduce the cross to a ticket to heaven that affects eternity but has little to say about today. Another possible reason is that, when it comes to the Christian life, many people simply resort to imitating Jesus as an example. Whatever the reason, the profound and multifaceted atonement theology of the church has too often been left in the books and left out of life.

May it not be! Theology is for all of life, infusing the church with a deeper understanding of the gospel in order to live faithfully as followers of Jesus. The good news of God's grace impacts all of eternity, but it also speaks to all of life, here and now. And while Christ is an example to be imitated, he is first and foremost a Savior to be trusted. The doctrine of atonement is essential for following Jesus and indispensable for the flourishing of the church.

How, then, does the doctrine of atonement apply to the Christian life?[2] While there are many ways to answer this question, I will argue that the key is union with Christ. As Paul says, "I have been crucified with Christ. It is no longer I who live, but Christ who lives in me" (Gal. 2:20). To live in light of the atonement, we must learn the crucial connection between Christ's work *for* us and Christ's work *in* us. The atoning work of Christ is applied and experienced through union with Christ by the Spirit.[3]

---

2. Of course, asking how the doctrine of atonement influences the Christian life already assumes a partial answer. Apart from the atonement, there is no Christian life. As oxygen is to breathing, atonement is to Christian living. Atonement does not merely affect life; it is the basis for new life.

3. Applying the atonement to the Christian life through union with Christ is not exclusive to other approaches that address the same problem. Moreover, I have tried to apply the doctrine of the atonement to the Christian life throughout this book. For example, the previous discussion about the vertical and horizontal dimensions of atonement has immense implications for the Christian life. But union with Christ is complementary, not contradictory, to this approach. As Paul says in 2 Cor. 5:19, God was reconciling the world to himself "in Christ," which means that vertical and horizontal reconciliation are not given to us *separate from* Christ or *in addition to* Christ but rather *in* Christ.

Atonement Accomplished and Applied

We begin with the distinction between atonement accomplished and atonement applied.[4] The Father sent the Son with a mission to save sinners and establish the kingdom of God. When Jesus cried out, "It is finished," from the cross (John 19:30), he made clear that he accomplished the mission for which he was sent. It is imperative, therefore, to understand and appreciate the *finished* nature of Christ's atoning work (Heb. 9:12, 24–26; 10:14). Jesus did not start a work that needed to be completed at another time. What he came to do, he did. And he did it perfectly and definitively. By dying sacrificially in place of sinners, Jesus fully accomplished all that is necessary for the salvation of people, the renewal of the cosmos, and the establishment of the eternal kingdom of God.

Why, then, if Christ's work is fully accomplished, is there still so much sin, suffering, and evil in the world? The answer is that while the finished work of Christ has been *accomplished*, it has not been fully *applied*. In between the "already" and the "not yet" of the kingdom of God, the Spirit must apply the finished work of Christ in and through his people. Christ's atoning work is not a partial accomplishment that needs to be finished but rather a full accomplishment that must be applied.

The distinction between atonement accomplished and applied is pivotal for John Calvin in his *Institutes of the Christian Religion*. After book 2, where Calvin lays out all that Christ has accomplished in his life, death, and resurrection, he begins book 3 by saying, "As long as Christ remains outside of us, and we are separated from him, all that he has suffered and done for the salvation of the human race remains useless and of no

---

4. I am drawing from John Murray's language in *Redemption Accomplished and Applied* (Grand Rapids, MI: Eerdmans, 1978).

value for us."[5] Could there be more shocking words to apply to Christ's glorious work than "useless and of no value"? But Calvin is right. Apart from union with Christ, sinners are left in utter dismay with no hope for the future. What is the solution, according to Calvin? "Christ effectually unites us to himself."[6]

The atoning work of Christ has already been accomplished— it is finished. But the finished work of Christ must be applied, and this happens through union with Christ by the Spirit.

Union with Christ

Apart from Christ, we have nothing. In Christ, we have everything. Our whole existence, therefore, hinges on union with Christ.[7] But what does "union with Christ" mean? At the most basic level, union with Christ refers to the idea that Christians are "in Christ" (2 Cor. 5:17) and Christ is in Christians (Col. 1:27). Constantine Campbell offers a more thorough definition, asserting that "union with Christ" is a meta theme encompassing the biblical ideas of participation, incorporation, representation, and union.[8] The mysterious nature of union with Christ, however, is precisely why the New Testament often uses analogies to discuss the oneness of Christ and his people:

- Jesus is the head; the church is the body (Col. 1:18).
- Jesus is the groom; the church is the bride (Eph. 5:31–32).
- Jesus is the vine; the church is the branches (John 15:1–11).

---

5. John Calvin, *Institutes of the Christian Religion*, ed. John T. McNeill, trans. Ford Lewis Battles, 2 vols., Library of Christian Classics (Louisville: Westminster John Knox, 2006), 1:537 (3.1.1).

6. Calvin, *Institutes*, 1:538 (3.1.1).

7. This is in reference to God's saving grace in Christ. His common grace, of course, is over all (Ps. 145:9).

8. Constantine R. Campbell, *Paul and Union with Christ: An Exegetical and Theological Study* (Grand Rapids, MI: Zondervan Academic, 2012), 29.

- Jesus is the cornerstone; the church is the building blocks (Eph. 2:19–22).

Jesus's message to his disciples captures the essence of union with Christ in a concise but profound way: "Abide in me, and I in you" (John 15:4).

Atonement Applied through Union with Christ

How, then, does union with Christ relate to the atonement? In short, all the benefits of the atonement are received in union with Christ by the Spirit. One of the most beautiful and potent portrayals of union with Christ in Scripture is Ephesians 1:3–11, which is one sentence in the original Greek and includes eleven references to believers being united to Christ.

The thesis statement of the passage is that "in Christ" God's people have been given "every spiritual blessing" (Eph. 1:3). The passage then goes on to praise God for the array of these blessings that the believer has in Christ: election, adoption, redemption, forgiveness, revelation, and so on. Furthermore, union with Christ applies beyond the individual. According to Ephesians, the entire story of the world will come to a head *in Christ*, the Savior who is not only reconciling sinners to God but is also uniting heaven and earth (Eph. 1:9–10).

Once again, it all depends on whether or not one is in Christ. Apart from Christ, we are . . .

- guilty in sin (Rom. 5:16);
- covered in shame (Jer. 17:13);
- deserving of God's judgment (Rom. 1:18);
- under the sway of the devil (Eph. 2:2);
- enemies of God (James 4:4);
- separated from God (Isa. 59:2);

- enslaved to sin (John 8:34);
- dead in transgressions (Eph. 2:1).

In Christ, we are . . .

- forgiven of sin (Eph. 1:7);
- cleansed of shame (Heb. 12:2);
- declared righteous (Rom. 4:5);
- victorious over the devil (Rom. 16:20);
- adopted into God's family (John 1:12);
- reconciled to God (2 Cor. 5:18–19);
- free from slavery to sin (Rom. 6:18);
- risen with eternal life (Rom. 8:11).

Everything hinges on union with Christ.

One of the most important implications of union with Christ is that it prevents Christians from seeking the benefits of atonement apart from the source of atonement—Christ himself. The greatest gift of God's grace is his own Son. The blessings of salvation do not come separate from Christ, nor are they in addition to Christ. The immeasurable riches of God's grace are given in Christ. As Bavinck says, "There is no participation in his benefits except by communion with his person."[9] The doctrine of union with Christ puts the emphasis on Christ himself while also celebrating all the benefits that come through him. The benefits of Christ's atoning work are not received from a distance but through Christ dwelling in the hearts of his people by the Spirit. This holds together the person and work of Christ—"Christ and him crucified" (1 Cor. 2:2)—as we experience God's grace in our lives. The work of Christ *for* us is received through the person of Christ *in* us.

---

9. Herman Bavinck, *Sin and Salvation in Christ*, vol. 3 of *Reformed Dogmatics*, ed. John Bolt, trans. John Vriend (Grand Rapids, MI: Baker Academic, 2003), 339.

The Role of the Spirit in Union with the Son

We have seen thus far that the accomplishments of Christ's atoning work are applied to sinners through union with Christ by the Spirit. Having spent much time discussing the role of the Son, I will now clarify the role of the Spirit. While the Spirit is active in every stage of accomplishing atonement (Rom. 8:11; Heb. 9:14), he is also—and especially—at work in applying atonement. This corresponds with the broad Trinitarian pattern in the Scriptures: atonement is planned by the Father, accomplished by the Son, and applied by the Spirit.

The role of the Spirit in applying the finished work of Christ is especially evident in the way the story of the gospel unfolds throughout the New Testament. After conquering death through death, the Nazarene carpenter walked out of the tomb and then ascended to the right hand of the Father. Sitting on a throne in heaven was a sign not only of Christ's finished work but also of his continual reign. How, though, does Christ reign from heaven? He reigns through the Spirit. Jesus poured out the Spirit on his disciples in order to apply his finished work, bringing about the renewal that would one day reach to the ends of the earth.

In the *Institutes*, Calvin's emphasis on union with Christ is coupled with the indispensable role of the Spirit. Calvin says, "[Christ] unites himself to us by the Spirit alone. By the grace and power of the same Spirit we are made his members, to keep us under himself and in turn to possess him."[10] The Spirit unites us to Christ whose finished work is then applied not in a transactional exchange but in a covenantal union (Rom. 8:9–10; 1 John 4:13). J. Todd Billings is right to say that union with Christ "has a trinitarian cast, as believers are united to Christ

---

10. Calvin, *Institutes*, 1:541 (3.1.3).

by the Spirit, who enables them to cry out to God as 'Abba! Father!' (Rom 8:14–17)."[11]

Dying and Rising with Christ

Union with Christ is not a static reality based solely on the person of Christ. It is a dynamic reality involving Christ's person and work. Believers are united with Christ in his death and resurrection (e.g., 2 Cor. 4:10; Phil. 3:10; 2 Tim. 2:11–12). Paul says, "For if we have been united with him in a death like his, we shall certainly be united with him in a resurrection like his" (Rom. 6:5). Union with Christ, therefore, means that not only are believers one with Christ but also they participate in his death and resurrection. Believers today are pulled into the historical events of Christ's crucifixion and resurrection.

Followers of Jesus, therefore, do not simply imitate Christ's suffering. We share in his suffering (Phil. 3:10). In a similar sense, the risen Christ does not merely bestow new life. We share in his life (Gal. 2:20). Mark Garcia says, "It is not enough that we died to sin like Christ; we have died to sin in and with Christ (Col. 2:9–3:4). Union with Christ is thus indispensable for the realism of the Gospel in its lived expression: we have died with Christ, we live in him."[12] By faith in Jesus, Christians are not merely following a pattern but rather participating in a reality—a covenantal union with the crucified and resurrected Christ.

Union with Christ teaches that the atonement is not only about Christ's work *for us* but also Christ's work *with us*. In more technical terms, a biblical understanding of atonement must give attention to the themes of substitution *and* repre-

---

11. J. Todd Billings, *Union with Christ: Reframing Theology and Ministry for the Church* (Grand Rapids, MI: Baker Academic, 2011), 10.

12. Mark A. Garcia, "Union with Christ," in *T&T Clark Companion to Atonement*, ed. Adam Johnson (New York: Bloomsbury T&T Clark, 2017), 784.

sentation. While Scripture affirms that Christ died in our place *instead of us* (substitution), it also declares that Christ died in our place *with us* (representation).[13] And Christ's representative work applies to the full scope of his ministry. We have been "crucified with Christ" (Gal. 2:20), "buried . . . with him" (Rom. 6:4), "raised with Christ" (Col. 3:1), and "seated . . . with him in the heavenly places" (Eph. 2:6).

The idea of representation is on display in the classic battle between David and Goliath. David fought as a representative of Israel. If David won, Israel won. If David lost, Israel lost. So when David defeated his giant foe, Israel shared in the triumph of their representative victor. Yet David points forward to his descendent, Christ. Jesus is the greater David who fought—as our representative—against our enemy, Satan. Though Christ is the one who wins the battle, his people share in his victory because he fought in their place as a representative.

It is not enough, therefore, to say that Christ died outside Jerusalem two millennia ago so that redemption could be applied to people here and now. There is a deeper reality at work. When Christ died on the cross, we died with him (2 Cor. 5:14). When Christ was raised from the dead, we were raised with him (Col. 3:1).[14] We are "fellow heirs with Christ, provided we

---

13. At this point, one may wonder what to make of the apparent contradiction between representation and substitution. If substitution, by definition, means exclusive place-taking, how then can Christ also be a representative who includes us in his work? On the one hand, we must affirm what Scripture teaches, and it clearly teaches that Christ is both our substitute and our representative. On the other hand, while the concepts may seem contradictory, they are not. As Simon Gathercole says, "Representation necessarily involves an element of substitution." Simon Gathercole, *Defending Substitution: An Essay on Atonement in Paul* (Grand Rapids, MI: Baker Academic, 2015), 20. Take, for example, a volleyball player who is a substitute in the middle of a game. By substituting for the other player, she takes her place on the floor. Yet, while she has taken her teammate's place on the floor, she still represents her teammate with her play. Substitution and representation are both at play and are not in contradiction. See also Campbell, *Paul and Union with Christ*, 351.

14. In this sense, John Murray's point is especially insightful: union with Christ "is not simply a phase of the application of redemption; it underlies every aspect of redemption both in its accomplishment and in its application." Murray, *Redemption*

suffer with him in order that we may also be glorified with him" (Rom. 8:17). Robert C. Tannehill says,

> If the believer dies and rises with Christ, as Paul claims, Christ's death and resurrection are not merely events which produce benefits for the believer, but also are events in which the believer himself partakes. The believer's new life is based upon his personal participation in these saving events.[15]

We participate in—without contributing to—Christ's death and resurrection. We bring nothing to Christ's atoning work except our transgression that makes it necessary.

Union with Christ shapes the doctrine of atonement in such a way that Christ is seen as substitute *and* representative. One need not choose between the two. As Jeannine Michele Graham concludes, "Jesus as Representative Substitute is seen both as exclusive place-taker in the sense of acting in place of sinful humanity while in another nuanced sense also as inclusive place-taker by acting on their behalf in a way that includes them."[16]

Atonement Experienced

To the categories of atonement accomplished and atonement applied, we add atonement experienced. Although the Spirit applies the finished work of Christ to the believer at conversion, it is still possible for believers to not feel or experience certain blessings that are truly theirs in salvation. For example,

---

Accomplished and Applied, 165. While it is helpful to make the distinction between atonement *accomplished* and atonement *applied*, representation helps hold them together in such a way that they are distinct but without division.

15. Robert C. Tannehill, *Dying and Rising with Christ: A Study in Pauline Theology* (Eugene, OR: Wipf and Stock, 2006), 1.

16. Jeannine Michele Graham, "Substitution and Representation," in Johnson, *T&T Clark Companion to Atonement*, 766.

though a believer is already forgiven in Christ, he or she may still choose to wallow in guilt. The Spirit, however, not only applies the finished work of Christ but also empowers believers to experience the benefits of the gospel in ever-deepening ways throughout their lives.

In 2009, an Israeli woman named Anat decided to surprise her mother by cleaning her apartment and getting her a brand-new mattress while disposing of the old one. What Anat did not realize, however, was that her mother had been storing her life savings inside of her old mattress and, by that point, she had saved one million dollars. By the time Anat and her mother realized what had happened, the mattress was buried in a landfill and could not be found.[17] Anat's mother had been sleeping on riches for much of her life yet was never able to truly experience the benefits.

Far too many Christians today are sleeping on the immeasurable riches of God's grace and, therefore, not experiencing the reality of what Christ accomplished for them in his atoning work. And unlike Anat's mother, these riches are not beneath them but rather in them. The good news of the gospel is that all the benefits of Christ's atoning work are *already* ours because the Spirit has united us to the Son. The Spirit takes what we know to be true in our heads and helps us to experience it in our hearts and in our lives.

Paul speaks of such an experience of the gospel in his prayer in Ephesians 3:14–21. He prays for the saints in Ephesus "to know the love of Christ" (Eph. 3:19). Of course, since he is writing this letter to "the saints who are in Ephesus" (Eph. 1:1), they are already intellectually aware of the love of Christ. Paul, therefore, is praying not merely for a cognitive knowledge of

---

17. Maev Kennedy, "Daughter Throws Away Mattress Stuffed with Mother's $1M Life Savings," *The Guardian*, June 10, 2009, https://www.theguardian.com/.

God's love but for an experiential knowledge of God's love. It is possible to know *about* someone without actually knowing them, but Paul wants Christians to know and experience God in a personal way.

Furthermore, Paul prays "that Christ may dwell in your hearts through faith" (Eph. 3:17), a clear reference to union with Christ. However, Paul has already made it clear in the book of Ephesians that they are in union with Christ (Eph. 1:3–14). So he is not referring in Ephesians 3:17 to an initial awareness of union at salvation, nor is he speaking merely of an intellectual knowledge of union. Paul is praying that they would experience what they know is true—that Christ really is dwelling in their hearts. With greater intimacy than husband and wife and a more vital connection than a head and a body, God desires not only for his people to *be* in union with Christ but to *experience* union with him. The Spirit leads the believer into a deeper awareness and experience of what he or she already has in Christ.

To experience the atonement, however, does not only involve feelings. Take, for example, the experience of reconciliation. Through Christ's atoning work on the cross, sinners are reconciled to God and to one another. The dividing wall of hostility has been torn down, and there is now a new united humanity, bound together by the blood of Christ (Eph. 2:14–16). This reconciliation—both the vertical and horizontal—is a gift of God's grace. As Kevin Vanhoozer says, "The church does not have to achieve reconciliation so much as display and exhibit the reconciliation already achieved through the death of Christ."[18] In other words, we do not work toward reconciliation but rather live into the reconciliation that we already have in Christ.

---

18. Kevin Vanhoozer, *The Drama of Doctrine: A Canonical-Linguistic Approach to Christian Theology* (Louisville: Westminster John Knox, 2005), 435.

I have shown how union with Christ helps apply atonement theology to the Christian life. But what does this look like in practice? We will now explore three truths that ungird much of the Christian's daily life: we share in Christ's identity, Christ's suffering, and Christ's mission.

Sharing in Christ's Identity

The most important question a person will ever answer is "Who is Jesus?" The second most important question, however, is inseparable from the first: "Who am I?" When it comes to identity, Jesus laid a foundation for his followers, and union with Christ is at the bottom of it.

For Christians, Jesus not only gives us a new identity but also invites us to share in *his* identity through union by the Spirit:

> Jesus is the beloved Son of God (Matt. 3:17).
> In him, we are children of God (John 1:12).
>
> Jesus is the light of the world (John 8:12).
> In him, we are the light of the world (Matt. 5:14).
>
> Jesus is a royal priest (Heb. 7:15–17).
> In him, we are a royal priesthood (1 Pet. 2:9).

The Heidelberg Catechism asserts that Jesus is called the Christ (meaning, "anointed one") because he is anointed as prophet, priest, and king.[19] The catechism, however, moves from the identity of Jesus to the identity of his followers. In explaining why a believer is called a "Christian," it demonstrates how those who are "in Christ" participate in Christ's threefold office:

---

19. "The Heidelberg Catechism," in *Creeds, Confessions, and Catechisms: A Reader's Edition*, ed. Chad Van Dixhoorn (Wheaton, IL: Crossway, 2022), 299–300 (Q. 31).

Because by faith I am a member of Christ and so I share in his anointing.

I am anointed to confess his name, to present myself to him as a living sacrifice of thanks, to strive with a free conscience against sin and the devil in this life, and afterward to reign with Christ over all creation for eternity.[20]

Union with Christ is the fountainhead for Christian identity. And this identity is shaped by the crucifixion and resurrection of Christ. In the Gospel of Mark, after Jesus is recognized as the Messiah (Mark 8:29), he goes on to redefine his identity as a King who will be crucified and resurrected. But what readers often miss is that each of Jesus's predictions of his crucifixion (Mark 8:31–33; 9:30–32; 10:32–34) is immediately followed by his teaching the disciples how they too are called to cruciform lives (Mark 8:34–37; 9:33–37; 10:35–45). To be in union with their crucified and resurrected Lord, the disciples must deny themselves, be servants of all, and use their influence for the good of others.

Sharing in Christ's identity is crucial for growing as followers of Jesus. Because we are given an identity in Christ, Christian growth is not a matter of changing into something you are not but is about becoming who you truly are "in Christ." In him, we are pure, holy, and righteous. Therefore, we are called to embrace our true identity by faith and to live out that identity in everyday life.

Sharing in Christ's Suffering

A true test of theology is whether it helps the church to suffer well. How can the doctrine of atonement alongside of union

---

20. "The Heidelberg Catechism," 300 (Q. 32). See also Zacharias Ursinus, *Commentary on the Heidelberg Catechism*, trans. G. W. Williard (1852; repr. Phillipsburg, NJ: P&R, n.d.), 178; Francis Turretin, *Institutes of Elenctic Theology*, trans. George Musgrave Giger, ed. James T. Dennison Jr., 3 vols. (Phillipsburg, NJ: P&R, 1994), 2:375–499.

with Christ speak to a cancer diagnosis, a broken marriage, or chronic physical pain? At one level, the doctrine of atonement teaches that Christ has accomplished all that is necessary for our full healing and that one day we will be delivered from all suffering. But in between the "already" and the "not yet" of the kingdom of God, suffering clearly plays a role in God's sovereign purposes. Union with Christ teaches at least three key truths about suffering in this life.

First, the Christian never suffers alone. When Christians suffer, we share in the suffering of Christ (Phil. 3:10). We "suffer with him" (Rom. 8:17). It is not enough to say that Christ modeled suffering for us. We do not merely suffer like him. We suffer *with* him. Furthermore, the Christian never suffers alone because our union with Christ includes a union with his body, the church. Followers of Jesus are called to "bear one another's burdens" (Gal. 6:2) and "weep with those who weep" (Rom. 12:15). This call to suffering together is exemplified in a beautiful way at the end of the book of Hebrews: "Remember those who are in prison, as though in prison with them, and those who are mistreated, since you also are in the body" (Heb. 13:3). One of the most difficult aspects of suffering is the isolation and loneliness that often comes with it. But because of union with Christ, the Christian never suffers alone.

Second, the Christian never suffers without purpose. Paul compares the suffering of humanity and creation to "the pains of childbirth" (Rom. 8:22). It is hard to imagine a better analogy than labor pains to prove the point that pain can have purpose. And while we cannot always know God's purpose in the moment (or season) of suffering, God has made clear his plan for eternity: the redemption of his people as part of his renewal of heaven and earth. From this perspective, Paul can affirm, "For this light momentary affliction is preparing for us an eternal weight of glory beyond all comparison" (2 Cor. 4:17). Notice that he does not merely say that affliction will be followed by glory. He says our affliction is "preparing for us" an eternal glory. The Greek word used for "preparing" (*katergazetai*) means "to bring about" or "to cause."[21] In other words, our affliction is producing for us something of eternal glory. And if we doubt this in our own lives, we need only look to the cross of Christ. The crucifixion is the greatest proof that God is working out his purposes in and through suffering. Because our suffering is with Christ, our suffering is never without purpose.

Third, the Christian never suffers without hope. Romans 8:17 says, "We suffer with him in order that we may also be glorified with him." And for this reason, Christians can face suffering with courage. Jesus said, "In the world you will have tribulation. But take heart; I have overcome the world" (John 16:33). We share in Christ's suffering and in his victory. And while the power of his kingdom is hidden beneath the cross in this age, we can also look forward to the full revealing of his glory in the age to come.

Charles Williams, a dear friend of J. R. R. Tolkien and C. S. Lewis, told a story from the early church of how union with Christ gives hope even amid the worst suffering imaginable.

> Her name was Felicitas; she was a Carthaginian; she lay in prison; there she bore a child. In her pain she screamed. The jailers asked her how, if she shrieked at *that*, she expected to endure death by the beasts. She said, "Now *I* suffer what *I* suffer; then another will be in me who will suffer for me, as I shall suffer for him."[22]

---

21. Walter Bauer, *A Greek-English Lexicon of the New Testament and Other Early Christian Literature*, rev. and ed. Frederick William Gingrich, 3rd ed. (Chicago: University of Chicago Press, 2000), s.v. "κατεργάζομαι."

22. Charles Williams, *Descent of the Dove: A Short History of the Holy Spirit in the Church* (Oxford: Oxford University Press, 1939), 28 (emphasis in original).

The kingdom was established through the suffering of Christ, and it is advanced through the suffering and service of those who are in Christ.

Sharing in Christ's Mission

After Jesus suffered on the cross and rose from the grave, he ascended into heaven to be seated at the right hand of the Father. But while Christ's atoning work is finished, his mission continues. In Acts 1:1 Luke refers to Jesus's entire earthly ministry (including his life, death, and resurrection) as "all that Jesus began to do." Reigning from his throne in heaven, the mission of Jesus carries on. Now, however, Christ's mission advances through the Spirit-empowered church. As Daniel L. Migliore says, "The missionary activity of the church should be understood as participation in the mission of Jesus Christ."[23]

Jesus saves. We do not. Yet we participate in his saving work as heralds of the gospel and witnesses to a better kingdom. Furthermore, just as Jesus was "mighty in deed and word" (Luke 24:19), we too are called to share in Christ's mission in both deed and word.

One key aspect of Christ's mission that we share is justice. Jesus came as the promised Messiah who would "bring forth justice to the nations" (Isa. 42:1) and who particularly focused his mission on the poor, the captives, the blind, and the oppressed (Luke 4:18). And through his atoning work and union by the Spirit, Jesus draws us into his work of justice:

> Christ has brought peace (Eph. 2:14).
> In Christ, we are peacemakers (Matt. 5:9).

---

23. Daniel L. Migliore, *Faith Seeking Understanding: An Introduction to Christian Theology* (Grand Rapids, MI: Eerdmans, 2004), 266.

Christ has achieved reconciliation (Rom. 5:11).
In Christ, we are ambassadors of reconciliation (2 Cor. 5:20).

Christ has established his kingdom (Mark 1:15).
In Christ, we witness to his kingdom (Acts 1:8).

To speak of sharing in Christ's mission of justice requires nuance, however, lest we confuse whose mission it is. J. Todd Billings explains:

> In ourselves, we are not the source of this good—our actions of justice are not the good news of the gospel. Rather, our actions that display love of God and neighbor reflect the gift of new life received in Christ through the Spirit. . . . This new life in union with Christ displays itself in a life of justice.[24]

The mission belongs to Jesus. But through union with Christ, we share in his mission.

A Greater Union

We have seen that union with Christ is the key to bringing one's understanding of Christ's atoning work to bear on the Christian life. All that Christ has accomplished for us in his atonement is applied through union with Christ by the Spirit. Furthermore, Christ not only died and rose *for* us, we also died and rose *with* him. Christ's work for us must be coupled with Christ's person in us. This nexus between atonement and union with Christ

---

24. Billings, *Union with Christ*, 108. Billings applies this to modern debates in a powerful way: "If we accept the claim that justice must ultimately be christologically defined as it is pursued in union with Christ, the liberal Protestant program of reducing the gospel to our acts of justice will not do. Neither will it do to fall into an evangelical reduction of justice to an optional add-on for Christians who want extra credit after properly performing 'essential' Christian duties that relate to the life of the soul" (115).

points toward a higher aim (union with God) within a broader story (the union of heaven and earth).

Union with Christ points to the even greater reality of participation in the life of the triune God. As Rankin Wilbourne says, "Union with Christ is the doorway to communion with God."[25] Second Peter 1:4 says that we will be "partakers of the divine nature," and according to 1 Corinthians 6:17, "he who is joined to the Lord becomes one spirit with him." One of the highest aims of Christ's work is that image bearers would be in union with their Maker. Yet even union with God comes within the broader story of the union of heaven and earth. Sin not only separated God and humanity but also rent asunder heaven (the dwelling place of God) and earth (the dwelling place of humanity). However, the renewing effects of Christ's atoning death reach as far as the effects of sin to which it is a response. The atonement brings about the union of God and sinners within the story of the union of heaven and earth.

---

25. Rankin Wilbourne, *Union with Christ: The Way to Know and Enjoy God* (Colorado Springs: David C. Cook, 2016), 85.

Conclusion

Behold, I am making all things new.
REVELATION 21:5

*The path of God is a daily cross. No one has
ascended into heaven by means of ease.*[1]
ISAAC THE SYRIAN

This book has put forth a view of the atonement as a multi-dimensional accomplishment within the story of the kingdom of God. While there are never-ending dimensions (healing, victory, propitiation, liberation, forgiveness, and so on), the heart of atonement is that Christ died as our substitute in our place and for our sins. That he died for *our* sins (not just *my* sins) is key, for community is not a mere implication of the atonement but rather is intrinsic to it. Furthermore, the doctrine of atonement ought to renew our minds and transform our lives. Through union with Christ by the Spirit, we are able to receive and experience all the blessings of Christ's atoning work, both now and forevermore. In short, I am advocating for a doctrine of atonement that is kingdom framed, substitution centered,

---

1. Saint Isaac the Syrian, *The Ascetical Homilies of Saint Isaac the Syrian*, trans. Holy Transfiguration Monastery (Brookline, MA: Holy Transfiguration Monastery, 2011), 59.

multidimensional, integrated, communal, life changing, and thoroughly Trinitiarian.

Made Whole

Kintsugi is a Japanese art form that takes broken pottery and puts it back together by sealing the cracks with gold. The result is not only a restored vessel but also a one-of-a-kind piece of pottery where the former places of brokenness are now accents of redemptive glory. That which was broken has been made whole. A pile of shattered pieces is made one and transformed into something even more beautiful than before.

Kintsugi offers a fitting picture of the atonement. Through his death on the cross, Jesus takes our broken lives and makes them whole again. And not only does he heal us as individuals and restore our communities, but he is also mending the cosmos. What holds us together, however, is not gold but blood. By offering his life in our place, Jesus heals our wounds and transforms our lives in such a way that we boast in our weaknesses because that is where his strength shines through. "We have this treasure in jars of clay, to show that the surpassing power belongs to God and not to us" (2 Cor. 4:7).

At-One

While Christ makes us whole again, the greatest accomplishment of the cross is that we are made at-one with God. And this is the key. If all the ills of the world were healed, all the injustices made right, and all the sadness undone, but we still were not right with God, then it would only be a momentary relief in our suffering and in our eternal longing for God. There are many problems in the world. But the atonement deals with the problem beneath every problem. Through Christ's death on the cross, we are reconciled to God.

Further Reading

Anselm. "Why God Became Man." Translated by Janet Fairweather. Pages 260–356 in *Anselm of Canterbury: The Major Works*. Edited by Brian Davies and G. R. Evans. Oxford World's Classics. Oxford: Oxford University Press, 2008.

Athanasius. *On the Incarnation*. Translated and edited by a Religious of C.S.M.V. Crestwood, NY: St. Vladimir's Seminary Press, 2002.

Bavinck, Herman. *Sin and Salvation in Christ*. Vol. 3 of *Reformed Dogmatics*. Edited by John Bolt. Translated by John Vriend. Grand Rapids, MI: Baker Academic, 2003.

Beilby, James, and Paul Eddy, eds. *The Nature of the Atonement: Four Views*. Downers Grove, IL: IVP Academic, 2006.

Cole, Graham. *God the Peacemaker: How Atonement Brings Shalom*. New Studies in Biblical Theology 25. Downers Grove, IL: IVP Academic, 2009.

Crisp, Oliver, and Fred Sanders, eds. *Locating Atonement: Explorations in Constructive Dogmatics*. Grand Rapids, MI: Zondervan Academic, 2015.

Green, Gene L., Stephen T. Pardue, and K. K. Yeo, eds. *So Great a Salvation: Soteriology in the Majority World*. Grand Rapids, MI: Eerdmans, 2017.

Hill, Charles E., and Frank A. James, eds. *The Glory of the Atonement: Biblical, Historical and Practical Perspectives; Essays in Honor of Roger Nicole*. Downers Grove, IL: IVP Academic, 2004.

Johnson, Adam J., ed. *T&T Clark Companion to Atonement*. New York: Bloomsbury T&T Clark, 2017.

McCall, Thomas. *Forsaken: The Trinity and the Cross, and Why It Matters*. Downers Grove, IL: IVP Academic, 2012.

McNall, Joshua M. *The Mosaic of Atonement: An Integrated Approach to Christ's Work*. Grand Rapids, MI: Zondervan Academic, 2019.

Stott, John. *The Cross of Christ*. Downers Grove, IL: InterVarsity Press, 1986.

Treat, Jeremy. *The Crucified King: Atonement and Kingdom in Biblical and Systematic Theology*. Grand Rapids, MI: Zondervan, 2014.

General Index

Scripture Index